CHRISTIAN PRESENCE SERIES
EDITOR: M. A. C. WARREN

❖

On the Eightfold Path

CHRISTIAN PRESENCE SERIES

GEORGE APPLETON

1344

On the Eightfold Path

>>> ❖ <<<

Christian Presence Amid

BUDDHISM

SCM PRESS LTD
BLOOMSBURY STREET LONDON

FIRST PUBLISHED 1961
© SCM PRESS LTD 1961
PRINTED IN GREAT BRITAIN BY
ROBERT CUNNINGHAM & SONS LTD
ALVA, SCOTLAND

General Introduction

>>> ✧ <<<

CHRISTIANS are being presented by the contemporary world with what is, in many ways, a unique opportunity of demonstrating the Gospel. Scarcely less unique is the opportunity being offered to them of discovering in a new and deeper way what that Gospel is. Those are large claims. Can they be justified?

What is this unique opportunity? At the very least it is the opportunity presented to Christians to demonstrate the fundamental truth of the Gospel that it is a universal message, whose relevance is not limited to any one culture, to any one system of thought, to any one pattern of activity. That is by no means the truism that it may appear to be. For more than four centuries the expansion of the Christian Church has coincided with the economic, political and cultural expansion of Western Europe. Viewed from the standpoint of the peoples of Africa, this expansion has been an aggressive attack on their own way of life. Quite inevitably the Christian faith has for many in these lands been inextricably bound up with this Western aggression. But it has also to be admitted quite frankly that during these centuries the missionaries of the Christian Church have commonly assumed that Western civilization and Chris-

5

tianity were two aspects of the same gift which they were commissioned to offer to the rest of mankind.

This assumption was sometimes quite conscious and was explicitly stated. More often it was quite unconscious and would have been indignantly denied. But in neither case are we called upon to judge our fathers. Their sincerity can hardly be disputed. Their self-sacrificing devotion finds its monument today in the world-wide diffusion of the Christian faith, the existence, in almost every country of the world, of a community of Christians recognizably part of the Universal Church.

What we are called upon to recognize is that in the world of our time there is a widespread revolt against any form of domination by the West. Nations whose political independence was only achieved 'yesterday' or is only about to be achieved 'tomorrow' can be excused for having their own interpretation of the past, an interpretation unlikely to coincide with that which is prevalent in the West. This very waning of Western influence is in part our Christian opportunity. We are freer today than we have ever been to serve the Gospel without the risk of confusion between that Gospel and the 'power' of the West.

But that is not all. The peoples of Asia and Africa, in their revolt against domination by the West, are presenting a specific challenge to the Christian faith. In what does this consist?

There are three main ingredients in this challenge.

First there is a critical evaluation of the Christian religion which rejects it as something inherently Western,

6

as something which fails to correspond to the *felt* needs of Asia and Africa. Christianity is, in such judgement, altogether too Western in its character and in the form which it assumes in its local manifestations. This rejection is the more serious in that Asian and African peoples are themselves, like us in the West, confronted by the bewildering demands of the modern world. All the old landmarks are disappearing. Everywhere there is a desperate search for some inner basis of security, some inner assurance which can enable men and women to face the storm. In the sequel, particularly in Asia, but not only there, the peoples of these countries are seeking to find this psychic security by digging deep into their own past. This is at once an expression of their revolt against the West and one explanation of the renaissance of the great ethnic religions. Further to this it is to be noted that in a new way these ancient religions are becoming themselves missionary. No longer content to be on the defensive, they are offering themselves as answers to the questionings of mankind.

Here is a situation which is new. Only once before, and then in its earliest centuries, has the Christian Church had to face a comparable challenge to its claim to meet the deepest needs of man's heart and mind. The devotees of Mithras, the mystery cults of the Mediterranean world, the Gnostics in that earlier day were serious competitors with the message of the Gospel. Their appeal failed. There followed the long thousand years during which Europe was isolated from the rest of mankind and built for itself its own peculiar civilization. Then suddenly, drawing on its inner dynamism, a dynamism closely related to its faith, the European world overflowed its narrow boundaries and began its great expansion. For a time it appeared as if nothing could arrest this expansion. It is of some importance to recognize that it is by no means certain that anything can! The scientific view of the world, with all its implications about human survival, is Western in origin. Communism and nationalism are Western concepts. It may well be doubted if anything can arrest the advance of all mankind towards something like a common civilization — if common destruction is avoided. Nevertheless there is, at the moment, a significant pause in the impetus of Western expansion in its Christian expression. The challenge to Christians is precisely this that the ethnic religions, as well as secularist philosophies of life, are offering themselves as the basis of the new world civilization. Both deny the relevance of Christianity.

The *second* challenge follows from the first. Can the Christian faith not only prove its ability to meet the deep human needs of our time but also make peoples of different cultural backgrounds feel at home in the new world? This is a more complex task than would appear. For it is part of our paradoxical situation that, at a moment when the world is becoming so obviously interdependent, every nation in it is seeking to assert its own independence. And religion and culture are the means by which independence is asserted. Has the Christian Church got a Gospel to meet this situation? We may put the question this way — can the Christians of the West

8

accept the fact that the expression which Christianity will receive in its Asian and African forms may well be, almost certainly will be, in many respects very different indeed from what we know in the West? That again could be worded as follows – are we of the West prepared to trust the Holy Spirit to lead the Christians of Asia and Africa, or must a controlling Western hand be permanently resting on the Ark of God? Let no one imagine that those questions will find an easy or unanimous response from Western Christians.

There remains a *third* challenge. The Christian Church has not yet seriously faced the theological problem of 'co-existence' with other religions. The very term seems to imply the acceptance of some limitation of the universal relevance of the Gospel. Can that be accepted? It can hardly be doubted that the answer must be 'no'. Are we then shut up to the alternative of what in some disguise or other must be an aggressive attack on the deeply held convictions of those who live by other faiths than our own?

This projected series of volumes has been designed to express a deliberate recognition of the challenge outlined above and to suggest that there is a way in which they can be met without any betrayal of the Gospel – indeed in deeper loyalty to that Gospel's real content.

First of the demands presented to us by this understanding of the contemporary world is a *glad* acceptance of the new situation in which the Christian faith can everywhere be distinguished from its past historical association with Western political, economic and cultural

9

aggression. Here is the 'great new fact of our time', every whit as great a fact as the existence of the Church in every land. Here is our great new opportunity, even though it may well be an opportunity to witness through suffering. The Cross, after all, was not a symbol of imperial domination but of the *imperium* of sacrifice. The Christian faith has nothing to lose by suffering. In and through suffering it can perhaps speak home to the hearts and minds of suffering mankind better than in any other way.

Second of the demands upon us, to march with our gladness, is a deep humility, by which we remember that God has not left himself without witness in any nation at any time. When we approach the man of another faith than our own it will be in a spirit of expectancy to find how God has been speaking to him and what new understandings of the grace and love of God we may ourselves discover in this encounter.

Our first task in approaching another people, another culture, another religion, is to take off our shoes, for the place we are approaching is holy. Else we may find ourselves treading on men's dreams. More serious still, we may forget that God was here before our arrival. We have, then, to ask what is the authentic religious content in the experience of the Muslim, the Hindu, the Buddhist or whoever he may be. We may, if we have asked humbly and respectfully, still reach the conclusion that our brothers have started from a false premise and reached a faulty conclusion. But we must not arrive at our judgment from outside their religious situation. We have to try to sit where they sit, to enter sympathetically into the pains and griefs and joys of their history and see how those pains and griefs and joys have determined the premises of their argument. We have, in a word, to be 'present' with them.

This is what is meant by the title of this series – *Christian Presence* amid Islam, Hinduism, Buddhism. . . . This will not be an easy approach. But then the love of God is not easy.

The second volume in this series treats of the Christian Presence amid Buddhism. The author, the Rev George Appleton, has known Buddhism at first hand in Burma and has maintained close links with Buddhists since his return to England. His approach to his subject, which is the approach of this whole series, is to discover first of all what Buddhism means to the thoughtful and sincere follower of the Eightfold path.

In order to make that discovery he takes the reader back to the teaching of Gautama, the Buddha, himself, letting him speak in his own words and interpret his own meaning, the while full use is made of the understanding of Buddhism by modern Buddhist scholars and writers.

All the while Mr Appleton is concerned to show that Buddhism is for the Buddhist a genuine attempt to find an answer to the riddle of human life, and in particular to the problem of evil as that expresses itself in the experience of pain. Again and again our author shows how closely the Christian seeker comes to his Buddhist companion, in proportion as both are grappling with the real challenges of human life.

Yet we are left in no doubt of the wisdom of a recent writer, a Japanese Buddhist, Professor Yoshinori Takeuchi, when he says that 'where there is an enhanced possibility of mutual appreciation there is also the increased risk of misunderstanding'. That may sound paradoxical but it is surely true to experience. Language may approximate. Insights may seem to be shared in common. But if the premises of thought are radically different only confusion will result from the over-easy assumption that we really are speaking about the same things. The same Japanese writer has agreed that 'there is a basic difference between the compassion of Buddhism and the love (*agapé*) of Christianity'. He goes on to add that this difference cannot be 'completely identified'.

Mr Appleton's most sensitive and sympathetic approach to Buddhism, to Buddhists, illuminates this difference, but it may confidently be claimed that he does so with a compassion that the Buddhist will recognize and with a love which will challenge the Christian reader to follow the way of understanding. On that road the Christian will encounter not only the Buddhist fellow-traveller but the Christ himself. When these three meet together it is not only the Buddhist who will be changed.

M. A. C. WARREN

Contents

Foreword

>>> ✛ <<<

DR KRAEMER in his great book *The Christian Message in a non-Christian World*, written in preparation for the Tambaram Conference of the International Missionary Council in 1938, said 'The real meeting between Christianity and Eastern systems of life has not yet taken place, and is still a matter for the future. All the work that has been done is preliminary, and nobody can tell how long this stage will last.' In a later book, *Religion and the Christian Faith*, published nearly twenty years later, he is quite sure that the real confrontation is about to take place.

Religions are being brought into encounter in a way that has not been possible before. The rapid development of communications has made it possible for people to move about the world more quickly; news and views travel from one part of the world to another in a matter of seconds; television brings the sight and sound of people of other religions into millions of homes. Nationalism has focussed the attention of people in Asia and Africa today on their own history and culture and on the traditional religion which has inspired their spiritual teachers in the past. The achievement of independence has brought people of other faiths to the lands of the

15

West for higher studies in universities and for service in embassies and in commerce. Religion is no longer determined by geography. Another factor in the growing encounter is the effect of the Christian missionary movement of the past 150 years, of which Professor Otto said as early as 1931 'The stir of new life in the great religions of the East . . . is largely a result, and a highly desirable result too, of the Christian missionary endeavour.'[1]

The result of all this has been revival in the great traditional religions of Asia, not only in the lands of their origin and early missionary expansion, but in new missionary activity in the West. The recognition that the world is in a mess arouses a desire to prove that the religion in question is one which can best get the world out of its unhappy predicament. There is also the impact of modern ideas, sciences and technology, the struggle between democracy and totalitarian systems, which are impelling the leaders of each religious faith to think out the relevance of their faith to modern conditions, with a consequent desire to catch up with the modern world.

In the lands of these religions the missionary movement has been transformed into a community of sister churches, no longer spiritual colonies of the West, but equal partners in world mission, seeing how the gospel is relevant to their own situation and accepting the responsibility of presenting the gospel to their own people and of taking their part in wider mission. At the fiftieth anniversary of the Edinburgh World

[1] R. Otto, *Religious Essays*, OUP.

Foreword

Missionary Conference of 1910, Bishop Newbigin said that there were no less than 200 Asian Christians serving in the Christian Mission outside their countries of birth.

In this new and exciting encounter, Buddhism is perhaps the most confident and vocal of the great religions. This book is an exercise in encounter, on the part of one who for the past thirty years has lived on the Christian-Buddhist frontier, and has often moved across it to listen to friendly Buddhists on the other side, in an effort to understand their experience and convictions. Inevitably that encounter results in musings and conversations about the similarities and the differences between the two religions. It has aroused in the writer's mind a genuine reverence for the Buddha and for the way of life which he set before his followers and the world. He has tried to put into practice the principle which Archbishop William Temple stressed so strongly: 'Whatever thoughts any human soul is seeking to live by, deserve the reverence of every other human soul . . . everything men believe deeply is worth studying sympathetically and deeply.'[1]

There is, however, another conviction equally strong in the writer's mind, that truth is a unity. To him it is axiomatic that all truth, goodness and love derive from one eternal source and will find perfection and fulfilment in that source. Again he must acknowledge his debt to Archbishop Temple: 'All that is noble in non-Christian systems of thought or conduct or worship is the work of Christ upon them and within them. By the Word of

[1] W. Temple, *The Universality of Christ*, SCM Press, 1921.

B

God – that is to say by Jesus Christ – Isaiah, and Plato, and Zoroaster and Buddha conceived and uttered such truths as they declared. There is only one divine light; and every man in his measure is enlightened by it.'[1]

So, as Temple Gairdner said in his book on the Edinburgh Conference of 1910,

Christianity, the religion of the Light of the World, can ignore no lights however 'broken' – it must take them all into account, absorb them all into its central glow. Nay, since the Church of Christ itself is partially involved in mists of unbelief, failing aspiration, imperfect realization, this quest of hers among the non-Christian religions, this discovery of their 'broken lights' may be to her the discovery of facets of her own truth, forgotten or half forgotten – perhaps never perceived at all save by the most prophetic of her sons.[2]

This last thought should keep Christians humble and guard them against any presumptuous claims. The Church as we know it is not yet fit to be the spiritual home of all religious men. The new encounter could make her so, if her conception of God is big enough to greet with joyful recognition his operation in other religions; if she is humble enough and patient enough to try to understand the other religions, and then to relate her gospel to theirs so that it comes to men of other faiths as good news in their own religious experience and conviction; if she will be universal in her outlook and not tied to any particular culture or organiza-

[1] W. Temple, *Readings in St John's Gospel*, Macmillan, 1945.
[2] W. H. Temple Gairdner, *Edinburgh 1910*.

18

tion, yet able to express her worship, faith and life in every culture and to be the inspiring spirit of every civilization; if she will call her children to put their Christian allegiance first and allow that to inspire their national patriotism, so that the brotherhood of man and the community of nations may be increasingly realized; if in her corporate life she becomes more like her Lord, with the humility of Bethlehem and the love of Calvary. The new encounter, then, will be one not only of energetic missionary activity and apologetic, but a transforming process which will help the Church to become the corporate expression of her Lord, who is the eternal expression of the Eternal God, he through whom God purposes to sum up all things – all men and all truth.

The plan of this book is simply a study of the Three Gems of Buddhism and of the Four Noble Truths in which the Buddha expressed his discovery and teaching. It is based mainly on Thera-vada Buddhism, the Teaching of the Elders, followed by Buddhists in Burma, Siam and Ceylon. In Christian terms we should speak of this earliest tradition as the Religion of the Early Fathers, as compared with Mahayana or Northern Buddhism which while accepting all the Scriptures of the Thera-vada School, collected many more of its own and developed doctrines not acceptable in the Buddhism of the South. Some reference is made in the course of this book to these developments, mainly as commentary on the points of Thera-vada under discussion.

The writer wishes to make several special acknowledgments of gratitude. First of all to Mrs Rhys Davids who first taught him to look for a gospel in Buddhism, which made men hail it as good news. Secondly to P. W. Martin who in his book *Experiment in Depth* gave him the clue to study the Buddha as the great pioneer in the study of human psychology. This clue led him back to Jung, whom Zaehner calls 'a new Buddha', and who in *The Secret of the Golden Flower* said:

I can say that my admiration for the great Eastern philosophers is as great and as indubitable as my attitude toward their metaphysics is irreverent. I suspect them of being symbolical psychologists, to whom no greater wrong could be done than to take them literally. If it were metaphysics that they mean, it would be useless to try to understand them. But if it is psychology, we can not only understand them, but we can profit greatly by them, for then the so-called 'metaphysical' comes within the range of experience. If I accept the fact that a god is absolute and beyond all human experience, he leaves me cold. I do not affect him, nor does he affect me. But if I know, on the other hand, that God is a mighty activity of the soul, at once I must concern myself with him.[1]

A third word of gratitude is due to Dr Coomaraswamy and Miss Horner for *The Living Thoughts of Gotama the Buddha*, one of the most in-seeing, interesting and human anthologies of Buddhist texts. A considerable number of the quotations from the Buddhist Scriptures included in this book come through that collection; the references given are those of Miss Horner and Dr Coomaraswamy to the original sources.

[1] C. G. Jung, *The Secret of the Golden Flower*.

Foreword

The relationship between religions seems likely to be a question of great significance in the period of history ahead. The hopes it arouses have never been better expressed than by Otto, who writing thirty years ago, said:

There is an immense struggle pending. Perhaps its greatest period will not occur until humanity has reached a stage of political and social equilibrium. Enviable is he who may see that day, for it will be the highest and most solemn moment in the history of mankind, when we shall no longer have political systems, economic groups and social interests but the religions of mankind pitted one against another, and when instead of futile contests regarding their accessories of myth and dogma we shall see the stage set for spirit to measure itself against spirit, ideal against ideal, experience against experience, when each will have to declare without reserve what he has that is profound and genuine, and whether he has anything.[1]

[1] R. Otto, *Religious Essays*.

1

The Setting

>>> ✧ <<<

'THERE is only one whom we might be inclined to
compare with Jesus: Buddha. This man is a great
mystery. He lived in an awful, almost superhuman
freedom. Yet his kindness was powerful as a cosmic
force. Perhaps Buddha will be the last religious genius
to be explained by Christianity. As yet no one has really
uncovered his Christian significance.'[1]

This small book may not succeed in doing that, but
it is the effort of one who for many years has lived in
thought on the frontier where Christianity and Buddhism meet, one who has a deep reverence for the Buddha
as one of the greatest born of woman, and believes that
any coherent view of divine activity in the world and
achievement within the human spirit must be able to
account for both Gautama and Jesus. 'Divine activity'
and 'human achievement': these two terms have
to be co-related. No more difficult or exciting a task
could be undertaken: not just to compare Gautama
the Buddha and Jesus the Christ but to relate them;
not just to compare Buddhism and Christianity as
independent and rival systems, but to seek the
Christian presence in Buddhism, and in the search to

[1] R. Guardini, *The Lord*, Longmans, 1956, p. 305.

23

discover inevitably a Buddhist presence in Christianity.

The Buddha was preoccupied with the pain, the futilities, the impermanence, the meaninglessness of human life; his aim was to discover a way of escape for men into a sphere of perfect being, where there was no more need of change and rebirth, of perfect blessing where there was no more pain, of deathlessness where there was no more aging and dying, a sphere of time-lessness and eternity. The urgent thing was to put before men this goal and show them the way that leads to it. In this age, at any rate, too much time was spent in discussing metaphysical questions which distracted men from the main task of holy living which alone could lead to the goal. Such was his conviction.

A typical example of this unprofitable speculation can be seen in the question put to him by a disciple, who complained: 'There are three problems unexplained, put aside and rejected by the Blessed One. Namely, (1) is the universe eternal, or (2) is it not eternal, (3) is the universe finite, or (4) is it infinite, (5) is the soul the same as the body, or (6) is soul one thing and body another thing, (7) does the Tathāgata (*the Buddha*) exist after death, or (8) does he not exist after death, or (9) does he both (at the same time) exist and not exist after death, or (10) does he both (at the same time) not exist and not not-exist?'[1]

The Buddha reminded his disciple that in calling him to discipleship he had never promised to answer such questions, and pointed out that the state of most men

[1] *Majjhima-Nikāya*, No. 63, Pali Text Society.

was as parlous as that of the man shot with a poisoned
arrow whose surgeon refused to pull out the arrow
until he knew who had shot the sufferer, to what caste
he belonged and all about his family and personal
appearance.

The Buddha saw equally little hope in the outward
ceremonies, the recitation of religious *mantras* or magical
formula, the system of sacrifices prescribed by the
Brahmans of his day. The Brahmans, who were the
highest of the four castes on which Indian life was
organized, were always at the court of the rajah as bard,
priest and sacrificer, they alone knew the right ceremonies for conception, birth, marriage and death, they
alone could use the Vedas and quote the Vedic texts;
they guarded the sacred fire in the temple or grove: they
alone could utter the right *mantra* and offer the effective
sacrifice. Brahmans thought of themselves as above even
kings; they were so by birth rather than worth.

The Buddha's attitude to them can be seen in the
following quotations from the *Dhamma-pada*, a collection of verses generally thought to contain the essence
of his teaching:

> *Whoever month by month should sacrifice*
> *for a century with a thousand (offerings),*
> *but should venerate even for a moment*
> *one who has made the Self become –*
> *that veneration is better than oblation for a hundred years.*
>
> *And whoever may tend for a century*
> *the (sacred) fire in the (sacrificial) grove,*

25

but should venerate for a moment
one who has made the Self become –
that veneration is better than oblation for a hundred years.

Not by matted locks, nor by lineage, nor by caste
is one a Brahman; he is Brahman in whom are
truth and righteousness and purity.

What boots your tangled hair, O fool, what avails your
garments of skins? You have adorned the outer parts, within
you are full of uncleanness.[1]

The Christian in reading these verses remembers the stern criticisms of Jesus of the religious teachers of his day 'who cleanse the outside of the cup and platter; but your inward part is full of extortion and wickedness' (Luke 11.39).

There is a fine passage in the *Anguttara-Nikāya* which speaks of the unworthy sacrifice of bulls, steers, heifers, goats, rams; the very intention of offering such a sacrifice is an evil thought-sword, the order to kill is a word-sword, the action of killing is a deed-sword, three weapons which will inevitably injure those who use them. Similarly, the worthy fire is the honouring of parents, family, workmen, the shunning of the evil fires of passion, hatred and delusion, the abstinence from pride, indolence, impatience.

The Buddhist shudders at the record of animal sacrifices in the Old Testament. Jews may comfort themselves in the thought that the sacrifice of the lamb symbolized the offering of the worshipper's own life, and Christians

[1] *Dhamma-pada*, 106, 107, 393, 394.

26

The Setting

may plead that the Christ's offering of his own life was the end of animal sacrifices, but the Buddhist will press the question, 'Was the Old Testament system of sacrifice men's devout but mistaken belief that God wanted animal sacrifices, or did God demand the bloody sacrifice of his creatures?'

In his attitude towards the Hindu cult of his time, the Buddha was akin to the great prophets of the Old Testament. How his heart would have warmed to the prophetical criticisms of Amos and Isaiah!

I hate, I despise your feasts, and I will take no delight in your solemn assemblies. Yea, though ye offer me your burnt offerings and meal offerings, I will not accept them: neither will I regard the peace offerings of your fat beasts. Take thou away from me the noise of thy songs; for I will not hear the melody of thy viols. But let judgement roll down as waters, and righteousness as a mighty stream.[1]

To what purpose is the multitude of your sacrifices unto me? saith the Lord: I am full of the burnt offerings of rams, and the fat of fed beasts; and I delight not in the blood of bullocks, or of lambs, or of he-goats. When ye come to appear before me, who hath required this at your hand, to trample my courts? . . . Wash you, make you clean; put away the evil of your doings from before mine eyes; cease to do evil: learn to do well; seek judgement, relieve the oppressed, judge the fatherless, plead for the widow.[2]

The Old Testament prophets, the Buddha and the Christ all agree that the only acceptable offering is holy living.

[1] Amos 5.21–24.   [2] Isa. 1.11–12, 16–17.

Yet there was something deeper and nobler in the religious climate of India in the time of the Buddha. In the earliest scriptures, the *Vedas*, the gods worshipped are the powers of nature. Gradually belief in the old gods decayed though the old worship and sacrifices continued; these details of ritual are preserved in a collection of books called the *Brahmanas*. As belief in the old gods decayed, a more philosophical type of religion developed in which men tried to probe into the ultimate reality at the heart of things. From this probing arose a third set of scriptures entitled *Upanishads* (literally sessions of instruction received at the feet of a master). The central philosophy of the *Upanishads* is that there is only one ultimate reality, *Brahma*, the all-in-all, the impersonal Absolute, beyond all human thought and language, which can only be described in negative terms *neti, neti*, not so, not so. Brahma is the great SELF of the Universe; Brahma is in man, and man is in Brahma and indeed is Brahma. The human spirit is one with the divine Spirit. This identity is expressed in two phrases *tat tvam asi*, That thou art, and *aham brahmasmi*, I am Brahma. When a man realizes this he achieves *moksha*, release. The whole discipline of yoga is designed to enable man to attain to this union with the divine. The *Upanishads* began to take shape about 800 B.C. and the process was probably still going on during the lifetime of the Buddha (*c.* 560-480 B.C.).

Two things perhaps need to be said about this new development of thought. The first is to acknowledge the daring and wonder of it.

28

The Setting

We do not know when it was that the gospel of immanent
Deity, of the Highest as being potential in the very nature
of each man and woman, in the nature of the 'man-in-man',
was uttered in India. . . . But it must have been at its in-
ception a new outbreathing of a wonderfully inspiring kind.
It may come trippingly over the lips of pundit and pupil
nowadays, but when considered in a quiet hour it is even
more tremendous for us than perhaps at its birth, so have
we grown, or so ought we to have grown in the concept of
Deity. And it must have, in any case, been a word of tremendous weight then. . . . It was too wonderful a thing to be
well made clear amid the values of the world, the aims, the
unquiet, the warring, the playing, the work, the troubles,
the futilities of worldly life. It was a matter needing quiet;
it was a matter calling for realization by each man for
himself.[1]

The second thing needing to be said is to question the
total identity assumed in discussion today by Hindus
and Christians alike. Mrs Rhys Davids, attempting to
reconstruct the thought of the Buddha in direct first-
personal speech, puts the question in these words:

And when some of us said that the *ātman* (man) and the
Ātman (Deity) were the very same, we did not mean that
the man was very Brahman now; we meant 'same in
nature'. To be That, he had to become, and that becoming
was for each the way through the worlds. . . .[2]

The New Testament speaks of the precious and exceeding
great promises of God and the divine power through
which 'ye may become partakers of the divine nature,

[1] Mrs Rhys Davids, *Sakya*, Kegan Paul, pp. 43f.
[2] Ibid., p. 52.

having escaped from the corruption that is in the world by lust'.[1] Here is a text which is relevant at a point where Hinduism, Buddhism and Christianity meet.

The teaching of the Buddha must then be viewed in the background not only of the dominant position held by the Brahmans, both in the courts of the rajahs and in the homes of the people, but also in relation to the central thought of the religious thinkers of his time, namely the immanent theism of the *Upanishads*. It is true that the Buddha said little about the existence of a Supreme Being, but the word 'Brahma' is used often in compound words, such as *Brahma-bhuto* Brahma-become. Theravada Buddhist writers claim that in the Pitakas 'Brahma' has no theistic significance, but if the Buddha used it it would certainly have a sense of immanent theism in the minds of his hearers. There may have been good reasons why the Buddha did not deal with the goal of Hindu aspiration: there may have been more pressing preparatory steps which had to be taken before the higher stages could be reached, a clearing away of superstition, a call to man to realize his own being and to exert his will to become that of which he was innately capable.

[1] II Peter 1.4.

2

The Buddha

>>> ✧ <<<

'BOTH now and heretofore I teach just this, ill and the end of ill.' This word of the Buddha brought under one dominating aim the two portions of his life: his early manhood until the age of thirty, as Prince Siddhattha, of the Gautama family, son of King Suddhodana of the Sakya clan, ruler of Kosala, a kingdom in the Ganges valley; and the succeeding fifty years as the Buddha, the Enlightened One, the Awakened One. The earlier period is marked by an anguishing awareness of the pain, impermanence and meaninglessness of human life; in the later period he proclaims a gospel, good news about the end of ill, the way of escape into an eternal sphere of perfect being and ineffable blessing.

Between the 'ill' and 'the end of ill' comes a period of six years of determined search, of trial and error. Sensitive to a high degree to the sufferings of others, the young rajput was even more troubled by the inevitability of disease, aging and dying. As a Hindu he believed in rebirth, which, unless something new happened in the life of man, meant only another cycle of disease, aging and death. What was the cause of it all? How could a way of escape be found?

In the pressure of such questions as these he deter-

31

mined to leave his wife and new-born child and the kingdom over which his father had hoped that he would rule, and became a *Bhikkhu*, a mendicant, a homeless one. First of all he placed himself under the guidance of Brahman hermits living the contemplative life, and when no light came from this effort, he underwent the most severe austerities, but realized that these practices were only weakening body and mind, and would not lead to the discovery of the cause of men's ill. So he returned to the mendicant life and begged his daily food from the homes of religious people in the villages and small towns through which he passed. At length he felt within him that the moment of discovery was near, so he sat down under the sacred Bodhi tree, the tree of knowledge, and determined to seek within himself the answer to his questions.

There followed a night of enlightenment and spiritual exaltation, in which he saw with new significance the whole story of his former births and gained the knowledge of the cause of ill and the way to stop the operations of that cause.

In that moment of exaltation he may well have uttered two stanzas preserved in the *Dhamma-pada*:

Many births have I traversed seeking the builder; in vain! Weary is the round of births. Now art thou seen, O Builder. Nevermore shalt thou build the house. All thy beams are broken; cut down is thy cornerstone. My mind is set upon Nirvana; it has attained the extinction of desire.[1]

The builder of the recurrent cycle of lives is desire;

[1] *Dhamma-pada*, 153–4.

the cause of all man's misery has been recognized. Until
now man's life has been like a wheel in a horizontal
plane, for ever revolving on its own axis without progress. Now that wheel is broken and another wheel
takes its place, the wheel of *Dhamma*, turning in a
vertical plane, moving forward through the worlds
towards the goal.

From this night of enlightenment onwards Gautama
is known as the Buddha, the Enlightened One, the
Awakened One, the One who knows. Another name
which he can now rightly claim is Tathāgata, 'Come
this far', the One who has arrived, i.e. has reached
Nirvana; this name is translated by some writers as
Truth-Finder, no longer one in search of truth as he
has been through the years of travail, but the One who
has found the Truth.

The Buddha summed up the truth that he had found
under four heads, spoken of by Buddhists as the Four
Noble Truths:

1. *Dukkha*, often translated by ill, suffering, pain, but these
words have too narrowly the sense of physical suffering,
whereas the term used by the Buddha has a much
wider sense, embracing the idea of impermanence,
imperfection, frustration, meaninglessness, emptiness,
unsubstantiality. So the Pali word will be retained.
2. *Samudaya*, meaning 'uprising', the cause or origin of
dukkha, which is desire.
3. *Nirodha*, meaning 'stopping', the cessation or ending of
dukkha, through the stopping of desire.
4. *Magga*, meaning 'the way', which leads to the ending of
dukkha, the following of the Noble Eightfold Path.

Having attained this insight of truth that the stopping of desire would result in the stopping of *dukkha*, and having experienced the ineffable peace and happiness that followed from it, the Buddha was tempted to enjoy it for himself, and to pass from Nirvana here and now, to *Pari-nirvana*, the Nirvana Beyond, total Nirvana, from which there is no returning and of which no description can be given. That Nirvana can only be experienced. Christians are reminded of St Paul's experience which he would not, perhaps could not, put into words:

I know a man in Christ . . . whether in the body, I know not, or whether out of the body, I know not; God knoweth, such a one caught up to the third heaven . . . and heard unspeakable words, which it is not lawful for a man to utter.[1]

The Buddha, however, resisted the attractive temptation. Compassion had always been a dominant feeling in his mind; his search had been for a way of escape for men, not for himself alone. Ever a realist, he recognizes in the moment of enlightenment and exaltation, that the mass of men will be indifferent, yet there will be some who will listen and understand. So he refuses to be a Solitary Buddha, awaiting the Final Nirvana. He will preach the Truth he has discovered, so that men may attain the ultimate purpose of life. Streeter comparing the Buddha and the Christ says, 'Each for the sake of miserable humanity made the supreme sacrifice – the Christ in submitting to death, the Buddha by consenting to live.'[2]

[1] II Cor. 12.2, 4.
[2] B. H. Streeter, *The Buddha and the Christ*, Macmillan, 1932, p. 42.

34

The Buddha

Western students of Buddhism have often described it as a religion of pessimism, but even a cursory study of the Four Truths should make clear that such a view is mistaken. Had the first truth stood by itself such a judgement might have been legitimate, as it is in the case of the writer of Ecclesiastes.

Vanity of vanities, saith the Preacher; vanity of vanities, all is vanity. What profit hath man of all his labours wherein he laboureth under the sun? One generation goeth, and another cometh; and the earth abideth for ever. . . . That which hath been is that which shall be; and that which hath been done is that which shall be done: and there is no new thing under the sun.[1]

To the Preacher in Jerusalem life was empty, meaningless, frustrating, with no onward progress about it, with the dark days of death ahead and no law which did justice to both righteous and wicked. The Buddha in central India was equally realistic about life as most men lived it, but he did not shrug his shoulders and regret that nothing could be done about it. By persistent determination he sought the cause of man's *dukkha* and a way to escape from it. His was a way of hope, a gospel of will.

The Buddha said very little about the existence of the Supreme Being, and in fact discouraged speculation about it. Never does he say in so many words, 'There is no God'; he is agnostic rather than atheistic. The question as to whether God exists or not is an unprofitable one; the urgent thing is for man to realize that the

[1] Eccles. 1.2–4, 9.

35

cause of his unhappy state is desire and therefore he must begin to prevent the arising of that cause and so avoid its consequences. The way to do this is simple but difficult: tread the Noble Eightfold Path of right understanding, right thought, right speech, right action, right livelihood, right effort, right mindfulness and right concentration. Here is a programme of will and action, of cause and effect, of sowing and reaping.

With his discouragement of argument about the existence of God it is clear that the Buddha did not claim to be God, or an incarnation of God or even to be inspired by God. He was a man, pure and simple, who by his own intelligence and effort gained a knowledge of what he called *Dhamma*, which modern Buddhist writers tend to translate as 'Truth', lived his life in accordance with that knowledge and so realized perfect freedom and attained to the full truth of Nirvana.

The Buddha constantly urged his followers to exertion of will; they were not even to rely on him:

You yourself must make an effort. The Tathāgatas are only preachers. The thoughtful who enter the way are freed from the bondage of Māra (the tempter).[1]

The Buddha is only an example, a teacher, a show-er of the way, one who has arrived at the goal, who can call back words of encouragement to his followers still struggling on the way.

It is enough for the young man of family who has gone forth through faith to stir up energy and think 'Gladly would I

[1] *Dhamma-pada*, 276.

36

be reduced to skin and sinews and bones and let my body's flesh and blood dry up if there came to be a vortex of energy so that that which is not yet even might be won by human strength, by human energy for the attainment of the striving.' . . . Wherefore stir up energy for the attainment of the unattained, for the mastery of the unmastered, for the realization of the unrealized. Thus will this, your going forth, become not barren but a fruitful and growing thing.[1]

The Buddha starts with man and deals with him practically, empirically, and experimentally. He might well have echoed the words of Alexander Pope:

> *Know then thyself, presume not God to scan,*
> *The proper study of mankind is man.*

He confined himself to man or man's experience as he moved through succeeding lives and worlds. He wanted him to have some knowledge of the goal, some kind of a map to guide him in his wayfaring and an under-standing of the will within himself which must be persistently developed if he is to reach the goal. The religious conditions in which he lived suggested too much reliance on priests and mantras, ritual and sacri-fice. Man's understanding of the divine THAT in the credal crystallization, THAT THOU ART, was not yet spiritual enough to be of any positive help in the needed development of man's will. Perhaps man needed to understand himself, the human THOU of the formula, before he could truly appreciate the divine THAT with which he was to identify himself.

'Work out your own salvation with diligence', im-

[1] *Samyutta*, ii, 27–29 (PTS).

presses the Buddha on his disciples. St Paul says much
the same thing to the Christians of Philippi. 'Work out
your own salvation with fear and trembling', but he
adds 'for it is God which worketh in you to will and to
work'.[1] To the Christian there is the fact of God, a
forgotten, ignored or rejected factor to the Buddhist.
The Christian believes that there is strength available
for man from an outside sphere, to stimulate his will
and reinforce his actions. Buddhists who have become
Christian should have a deeper appreciation than other
Christians of one of the most familiar collects of the
Book of Common Prayer

Stir up, we beseech thee, O Lord, the wills of thy faithful
people; that they, plenteously bringing forth the fruit of
good works, may of thee be plenteously rewarded.[2]

How then may a Christian who reverently admires
the Buddha assess his greatness? Monsignor Guardini,
discussing the possible influence of one man on another,
says:

There is a limit to man's possibilities: he can affect only
things within the world . . . he cannot change the world as
a whole, for he is part of it. . . . He has no influence over
being as such, or its characteristics. He can change all
manner of things on the surface of the earth; earth itself
escapes his power. Only one person ever seriously attempted
to go further: to lay hands on being – Buddha. He attempted

[1] Phil. 2.12–13.
[2] *Book of Common Prayer*, Collect for the 25th Sunday after
Trinity.

the inconceivable: himself part of existence, he tried to lift all existence by its 'bootstraps'.[1]

May we not say that the Buddha is the highest point that human nature in its own wisdom and effort can reach. He was a giant among men, and the great statues in the pagodas of Pagan, the creative flowering of Burma's acceptance of Theravada Buddhism, and the great footmark on Adam's Peak in Ceylon, are symbols of the greatness which two Buddhist nations ascribed to him.

Jesus in his assessment of the religious history of his own people said:

Verily, I say unto you, Among them that are born of women there hath not arisen a greater than John the Baptist.[2]

The Christian in the thought of the self-emptying of the incarnate life of the Eternal Christ and of his acceptance of the limitations of human life and knowledge, would dare to put the Buddha in the same category of 'the greatest born of women'. Yet with his Master he would say that there is something beyond that. And the idea of a Beyond is as valid in Buddhism as in Christianity.

[1] R. Guardini, *The Lord*, pp. 305f.   [2] Matt. 11.11.

3

Dhamma

>>> ✧ <<<

D*hamma* is a difficult word to translate into English:
the Law, the Teaching, the Doctrine, the Norm, the
Truth have all been used. It is the principle of order
both in the Universe and in the moral sphere, a fusing
of the rational and ethical elements. It is that which
ought to be done, that which is established as obligatory.
'The whole duty of man' is as good a phrase as any to
express its comprehensive meaning. It comes very close
to St Paul's inward law, to the 'daimon' of Socrates, to
conscience; it is almost an inner light.

'Make what is right become' is the Buddha's bracing
word to Ananda.

Dhamma is not something which originated with
Gautama, it is something which earlier Buddhas
honoured and lived under.

> *The Perfect Buddhas who have passed,*
> *The Perfect Buddhas yet to come,*
> *The Perfect Buddha who is now,*
> *And hath for many banished woe –*
> *All dwelt true* dhamma *honouring,*
> *Do dwell and shall dwell: 'tis their way.*
> *So he to whom the Self is dear,*
> *Who longeth for the Great Self – he*

Dhamma

Should homage to true dhamma *pay,*
Remembering the Buddha-word.[1]

After his enlightenment the Buddha set in motion the wheel of *Dhamma* in his first sermon at Benares. When he sent out his disciples to preach they were to teach Dhamma.

Walk, monks, on tour for the blessing of the many-folk, for the happiness of the many-folk, out of compassion for the world, for the welfare, the blessing the happiness of *devas* and men. Let not two of you go by one way. Monks, teach *dhamma* which is lovely at the beginning, lovely in the middle, lovely at the ending. Explain with the spirit and the letter the Brahma-faring which is completely fulfilled, wholly pure. There are beings with little dust in their eyes who, not hearing *dhamma*, are decaying, but if they are learners of *dhamma*, they will grow. And I, monks, will go along to Uruvelā, to the Camp township in order to teach *dhamma*.[2]

At that time there was no written Dhamma in existence; to these first missioners there was as yet no set form of words, no system of doctrine.

When the Buddha lay dying, his devoted attendant Ananda asked for instructions concerning the Order of the Sangha. The Buddha's reply was that he had ever taught Dhamma, and Dhamma must therefore be their light and guide.

Therefore, Ananda, dwell making yourselves your island,

---

[1] *Anguttara-Nikāya* (PTS), ii, 20, 21.   [2] *Vinaya*, i, 20–21.

making yourselves, not anyone else, your refuge; making *Dhamma* your island, *Dhamma* your refuge, nothing else your refuge.[1]

They are to depend on Dhamma only, revere Dhamma, esteem Dhamma, with Dhamma as their banner, with Dhamma as their guard and protection, with mastery in Dhamma.

Dhamma is for awakening, for taming, for calming, for crossing over, for utter Nirvana.

Dhamma is the charioteer that drives the chariot along the road to Nirvana. In other references Dhamma is the raft on which men may cross the ocean of existence to the farther shore of Nirvana.

Dhamma is the master principle in '*a Tathāgata*, perfected one, wholly awakened one, a dhamma-man, a dhamma-king, depending on dhamma only, honouring dhamma, revering dhamma, esteeming dhamma, with dhamma as his standard, with dhamma as his banner, with mastery as to dhamma', and he will provide dhamma-guard, love and protection for monks, nuns and lay followers. He will do this by teaching the right kind of deeds, speech and thought, the right way of living, even the right places to visit or live in.

Similarly a king devoted to dhamma will provide a dhamma-guard for all within his kingdom – brahmans, soldiers, householders, recluses, town and countryfolk, even for beasts and birds.

Whoever wants to see dhamma in action has only to

[1] *Digha-Nikāya* (Colombo), pp. 61–62, quoted in Rahula, *What the Buddha Taught*, Gordon Fraser.

look at the Buddha himself: 'Whoever sees dhamma sees me, whoever sees me sees dhamma.' 'Monks, even if a monk should take hold of the edge of my outer cloak, and should walk close behind me, step for step, yet if he should be covetous, strongly attracted by pleasures of the senses, malevolent in thought, of corrupt mind and purpose, of confused recollection, inattentive, not contemplative, scatter-brained, his sense faculties uncontrolled, then he is far from me and I from him.'

Dhamma is as frequently on the lips of the Buddha as 'the Kingdom of God' is on the lips of Jesus. This latter concept was defined by Dr Hort as 'the world of invisible laws by which God is ruling and blessing his creatures'.

Yet the Kingdom is something which a man may have as an inner possession. It is a treasure worth selling everything else to get, a pearl of great price, incomparable in beauty and value. The contemporaries of Jesus thought of the coming of the Kingdom as an event to take place at some definite date in the future, to which Jesus replies that it is an ever-present and inner reality: 'The Kingdom of God cometh not with observation: neither shall they say, Lo, here! or there! for lo, the Kingdom of God is within you.' In other parables Jesus speaks of the Kingdom as a seed, which is to be sown in the soil of a man's being and which has infinite capacity for growth.

As in the time of Jesus, so in the time of the Buddha there were promising and unpromising souls in which the seed was to be sown. One day a headman asked the

Buddha why he taught Dhamma in full to some, but not to others.

The Buddha's reply was in the form of a parable of a farmer who had three fields, one excellent, one mediocre and one poor, which he would sow in that order. The excellent field represents the monks and nuns to whom the Buddha first teaches dhamma; the mediocre field represents lay-followers, and the poor field the recluses, brahmans and wanderers of other sects. Even the poorest field must be sown with dhamma 'because if even they were to understand perhaps even a single sentence, that would be a happiness and blessing to them for a long time'.

Jesus in the parallel parable of the Sower says 'the seed is the word of God'. In the Old Testament, *Torah*, the Law of the Lord, has the same double quality, something external and objective yet at the same time inner and creative. The prophet Jeremiah looked forward to a new covenant in which God would put his law in the inward parts of his people and write it in their hearts. In the time of Jesus the interpretation of the Law had become formal and static, no longer something living and almost personal as it had once been. Later Judaism, possibly in reaction to the criticism of Jesus, has recovered the living, dynamic sense of Torah, as something which can speak to new situations, with a life and dynamic of its own.

Buddhists and Jews may one day engage in dialogue about their respective conceptions of Dhamma and Torah, about the parts played by Moses and Gautama in the development of each, and about the spiritual source and authority behind each, which the Jew makes explicit in his faith in the Living God, but about which the Buddhist is silent. Dhamma is as dear to the Buddhist as Torah is to the Jew, and the former will understand something of what the Jew and Christian mean when they recite Psalm 19:

The law of the Lord is perfect, restoring the soul:
The testimony of the Lord is sure, making wise the simple.

The precepts of the Lord are right, rejoicing the heart:
The commandment of the Lord is pure, enlightening the eyes.

The fear of the Lord is clean, enduring for ever:
The judgments of the Lord are true, and righteous altogether.

More to be desired they are than gold, yea, than much fine
    gold:
Sweeter also than honey and the honeycomb.

Moreover by them is thy servant warned:
In keeping of them there is great reward.[1]

We have seen that there are passages in the Pitakas which speak of Dhamma as something which existed before the Buddhas, which is something within man guiding him along the right road, something which grows within a man and produces a harvest of holy living. It has an existence and reality of its own, the sense almost of an eternal principle.

The Buddha's last words to his disciples were to make

[1] Ps. 19.7–11.

45

both Dhamma and themselves their refuge, suggesting both an outer and an inner meaning, something that has not only an objective reality but an inner dynamic also. Dhamma is the permanent standard to which the Buddhist brings everything in judgement, the ideal to which he also appeals, the arbiter of values and the purpose towards which those values are directed. And it is the Buddha's exposition of the meaning and application of Dhamma which the devout disciple reveres, a reverence attested by the constant repetition in the Scriptures of the phrase 'the Dhamma of the Buddha'. But as in a number of other things, Buddhists take the reality of Dhamma for granted and do not go on to ask questions about its source.

Christians in Ceylon have made the question of the origin of Dhamma with its objective and subjective nature one of their main talking points with Buddhists:

The Dhamma does not merely mean the teaching of the Buddha. It is far more than that. It is the order of Law of the universe, eternal, uncreated. The Buddha as well as the previous Buddhas were only discoverers of the Dhamma. They were able to discern an eternal orderly principle of the universe in which the rational and the ethical elements were fused into one. Dhamma is rationality: anything as it should be according to its reason and logic. It is the ideal that is the norm of reason and morality.

When we reach this stage in the scale of values, we are confronted with what is called the 'antinomy of the ideal'. On the one hand we see that this ideal – Dhamma – or any other ideal, can be real only as a concept and acknowledged purpose of minds. This is why Dhamma is described in terms of rationality. It exists only in mind. On the other hand, the ideal is an objective norm and therefore external to persons. How can this antinomy be resolved?

This can be done in one of two ways. Either the Dhamma must be thought of as pure mind – the objective source and sustainer of values – or we should posit a supreme mind which is the source and sustainer of the Dhamma. Whatever alternative we accept, we would see that both point to the same object that religious worshippers have found, namely a supreme Being in whom the highest ideals are acknowledged and actualized. If there is nothing beyond the Dhamma, then the Dhamma must be that supreme Being.[1]

In the development of Buddhist teaching Dhamma came to be formulated in sayings, sermons, summaries of rules and doctrine, and in so doing it lost much of its inner dynamic character. Later Buddhism was much given to the analytical method, and in the process of enumeration much of the life seemed lost. Yet Dhamma has been retained as one of the three precious gems to which every Buddhist expresses his reverence before he begins his meditation:

> I go for refuge to the Buddha.
> I go for refuge to the Dhamma.
> I go for refuge to the Sangha.

As long as this is so there is hope that he may recover the original meaning of a word which, more often than any other term in Buddhism, was on the lips of the Blessed One, the first object of reverence. In the growing encounter between Christians and Buddhists the question of the origin of this eternal principle will be one of the main points of discussion.

[1] Lynn A. de Silva, *Belief in God*, CPCL Pamphlet, Colombo.

4

Dukkha: The Fact of Pain

>>> ✧ <<<

WHAT is the Noble Truth of Pain? It is, birth is pain, aging is pain, sickness is pain, death is pain, union with unpleasant things is pain, separation from pleasant things is pain, not getting what one wants is pain; the body is pain, feeling is pain, perception is pain, mental activity is pain, consciousness is pain, in short all grasping at any of these five groups is pain.[1]

Dukkha does not mean just physical pain, but pain of heart and mind as well — all dis-ease, strain, anxiety, frustration. The Buddha taught that human life is marked by the characteristics of imperfection, impermanence, emptiness, lack of abiding reality and permanent value. Sometimes this first truth is summarized in the words 'all is suffering', as if to suggest that there is nothing but suffering; it would be better to say that in everything there is the element of suffering, as interpreted above.

Many Buddhists and non-Buddhists think that the strength of Buddhism lies in its mechanistic explanation of the problem of suffering: present suffering is the result of wrong actions in the past, the past of this

[1] *Mahavasta*. Translation by E. J. Thomas, *The Quest of Enlightenment*, a selection of the Buddhist Scriptures.

present life or the past of earlier lives. They attempt to explain all the inequalities, sufferings and misfortunes of life in this way; as the consequence of past actions.

Much of one's present state is indeed the result of ignorant thinking or mistaken deeds in the past. But not all suffering can be so explained. There is a suffering that is caused by our solidarity with our fellow-men: a nation in time of war, the people of an area in time of famine or epidemic. Can one believe that all the people of Hiroshima were merely experiencing the consequence of past lives in the death-dealing destruction of the first atom bomb? Must not the authorities who decided to drop that bomb and the men who dropped it bear some moral responsibility, and indeed those who ordered the aggression of Pearl Harbour which brought war to East Asia? Certainly we can see the on going consequences of that action in human suffering and in the universal threat and fear of nuclear warfare.

Is there not also undeserved suffering voluntarily accepted, inflicted by the opponents of a man's way of life or of the principles by which he thinks nations should live? Was the death of Mahatma Gandhi in India, of Aung San in Burma, of Liaquat Ali Khan in Pakistan, or Bandaranaike in Ceylon, the due reward of their past deeds? It was certainly the consequence of convictions and policies, but surely not the working out of evil done in the past.

The Jews were faced with the same problem of suffering and for centuries were 'popularly Buddhistic' in their thinking. A man enjoying prosperity and dying peacefully in his bed was assumed to be receiving the just reward of a righteous life. For the man undergoing great misfortune and suffering or dying a violent death, an attempt was always made to find a crime to fit the punishment, a much more doubtful practice than that of Gilbert's Mikado.

The Book of Job is a moving protest against the popular interpretation that all suffering is the consequence of sin. Job knows that he is not perfect, but he can see nothing in his past that deserves the chain of shattering misfortunes that has fallen on him. He maintains this integrity against friends and critics who press the conventional view. Yet Job never solves the problem that has nagged at his heart all through his sufferings; his experience of God and the other mysteries of human life make a solution unnecessary. He is content to live with his problem, because he has seen God and heard him speak within his own being. The happy ending to the Book of Job which one is sometimes tempted to regret as unrelated in logic to the argument of the book, is evidence of the faith of the writer, or perhaps of the editor, that God will not leave things as they are. Job cannot be left repenting in dust and ashes; the story is not yet finished. There is something beyond, which will explain present happenings and set them right: the relation between right living and reward will only become clear when it is linked with the eternal order of things.

A further advance in spiritual thinking about human suffering is seen in chapter 53 of the Book of Isaiah, the poem on the Suffering Servant, in which observers who

Dukkha: The Fact of Pain

had witnessed the life of this unnamed sufferer see his life and death in a new light. They had thought him to be of little account, there was nothing powerful or attractive about him as men would think. He had borne opposition, persecution and death, without bitterness or self-pity, and people had thought that all this was God's punishment for his sins. But now they come to see that there was something redemptive about his sufferings, which in some mysterious way was to change people's hearts and win forgiveness for them.

because he poured out his soul unto death, and was numbered with the transgressors; yet he bare the sin of many, and made intercession for the transgressors. . . . He shall see of the travail of his soul and be satisfied. . . . Therefore will I divide him a portion with the great, and he shall divide the spoil with the strong.[1]

Buddhism knows much of sacrifice for others, both in the conception of the *Bodhi-sat* in Northern Buddhism who defers his entry into Nirvana for the sake of men, and in the spiritual fables of the *Jatakas*, the Birth Stories, which picture often in a childlike way, but sometimes with telling maturity, the sacrifices undergone by the Buddha in earlier lives. Neither Bodhi-sats nor Jatakas may be historical, but they are evidence of a conviction within Buddhism that sacrifice is both right and effective.

Jesus identified himself with sinful men when he stood in the Jordan to receive the baptism of repentance from John the Baptist. On the Cross he prayed for those

[1] Isa. 53.12, 11.

who had brought him there. Even when tempted to feel that God had deserted him his thoughts go to the opening verse of Psalm 22, 'My God, my God, why hast thou forsaken me?', a poem uttered by an earlier sufferer and ending with words of triumphant faith

All the ends of the earth shall remember and turn unto the
  Lord:
And all the kindreds of the nations shall worship before thee.
For the kingdom is the Lord's: and he is the ruler over the
  nations.[1]

But, as I have said, Buddhism has an understanding of sacrifice, and one day Buddhists will relate the sacrifice of Jesus to that understanding. It is the popular mis-interpretation of the more obvious sufferings of life which I have been criticizing. In the First Noble Truth there is a deeper and more realistic diagnosis of suffering as tension, anxiety, disharmony, frustration, meaning-lessness, transience. Perhaps our generation can appre-ciate this more deeply than any before. Two world wars have disillusioned men from the optimistic beliefs of the nineteenth century, we see that the great advance in human knowledge is no guarantee that men will become spiritually wiser, nobler in character and more just and loving in their relationships with their fellow men. The new discoveries, whether in the physical world or within the mind of man, make equally greater possi-bilities for evil as well as for good.

The Buddha's first Truth is one that was recognized by William James when, applying the scientific method

[1] Ps. 22.27–28.

52

Dukkha: The Fact of Pain

to the study of *The Varieties of Religious Experience* he formulated his first conclusion in the words 'there is something wrong about us as we naturally stand'. He, too, went on to three other truths, which will be mentioned in a later chapter.

T. S. Eliot in some of his poems written after the first world war shows something of the desolation and emptiness of modern life, haunted by memories of the past, and waiting for the knock of death upon the door. Like the old guy of children as November 5th approaches:

> *We are the hollow men*
> *We are the stuffed men*
> *Leaning together*
> *Headpiece filled with straw. Alas!*
> *Our dried voices, when*
> *We whisper together*
> *Are quiet and meaningless*
> *As wind in dry grass*
> *Or rats' feet over broken glass*
> *In our dry cellar.*

Within the heart of man there is the barren desolation of a desert:

> *This is the dead land*
> *This is the cactus land*
> *Here the stone images*
> *Are raised, here they receive*
> *The supplication of a dead man's hand*
> *Under the twinkle of a fading star.*

Something always seems to get between man and the achievement that he longs for:

> *Between the conception*
> *And the creation*

Between the emotion
And the response
Falls the shadow.

Between the desire
And the spasm
Between the potency
And the existence
Between the essence
And the descent
Falls the shadow.[1]

And the world ends in mumbling incoherence 'not with a bang but a whimper'.

Many young people today, in this country and perhaps more so on the Continent, are tempted to think of life as a nightmare of meaninglessness. Their frustration and tension were well understood by that king in Jerusalem with his 'Vanity of vanities, all is vanity'; by Marcus Aurelius with his 'Up and down, to and fro, round and round; this is the monotonous and meaningless rhythm of the Universe'; by T. S. Eliot in *The Waste Land* and *The Hollow Men*. The last-named entitles one section of the first poem 'The Fire Sermon', a deliberate reference to the Buddha.

It was the Buddha who in the First Noble Truth faced realistically and creatively the emptiness and meaninglessness of human life. The problem has been stated, the disease has been diagnosed: now he can proceed to track down the cause and prescribe a cure.

[1] T. S. Eliot, 'The Hollow Men' in *Collected Poems 1909–1935*, Faber and Faber.

54

5

The Doctrine of Non-Self

>>> ✧ <<<

BEFORE we go on to the Buddha's solution of the problem, however, it is necessary to study one central emphasis in the Buddhist interpretation of *dukkha*. One of the three characteristics of human life as described by the Buddha was *An-atta*, meaning no-Self, no-Soul, non-substantiality. Most Buddhists of the Theravada School interpret this as meaning that there is no such thing as self or soul or personal entity, which continues from one life to another and finally enjoys the blessing and perfected being of Nirvana.

Nyanaponika Thera, a German monk of Ceylon, describes 'belief in a self, a soul, or an eternal substance of any description' as 'the deepest and most obstinate delusion in man'.[1]

Walpola Rahula, another Buddhist writer from Ceylon, is equally explicit:

Buddhism stands unique in the history of human thought in denying the existence of such a Soul, Self, or *Ātman*. According to the teaching of the Buddha, the idea of self is an imaginary, false belief which has no corresponding reality, and it produces harmful thoughts of 'me' and 'mine', selfish desire, craving, attachment, hatred, ill-will, conceit,

[1] Nyanaponika, *The Heart of Buddhist Meditation*, Colombo, p. 35.

pride, egoism, and other defilements, impurities and problems. It is the source of all the troubles in the world from personal conflicts to wars between nations. In short, to this false view can be traced all the evil in the world.[1]

These modern writers have strong support from Buddhaghosa, the great commentator of the fifth century A.D.:

> *Mere suffering exists, but no sufferer is found;*
> *The deeds are, but no doer is found.*

Suffering but no sufferer, deeds but no doer, thought but no thinker, effort but no willer. Does not this make nonsense of any sense of responsibility in man or of any appeal to him to exert himself, to will the true thought or the good deed which shall be creative of future blessing? According to Buddhists the constituents of being are the five *Khandas* – *rūpa*, form or matter, body; *vedanā*, sensation, feeling; *saññā*, perception; *samkhāra*, mental activities; *viññāna*, consciousness. When these five aggregates are in combination there is life, a 'being' is in existence, though the aggregates themselves are impermanent and always changing. When these aggregates disintegrate death takes place.

In a discourse known as 'the Marks of Non-Self' the Buddha asserted:

Body, monks, is without self; feeling, perception, the other mental elements and consciousness are without self . . . whatever body there is, internal or external, coarse or fine,

[1] Rahula, *What the Buddha Taught*, Gordon Fraser, p. 51.

The Doctrine of Non-Self

base or lofty, far or near, past or present or future, all that body is not mine, I am not that, that is not the self.[1]

Similarly, feeling, perception, mental elements and consciousness are not the self. The Buddhist deduction from this is that there is no self. But is this the only possible deduction? Might not the Buddha have been saying — the self is not the body nor perception nor feeling nor mind nor consciousness, nor even all these in combination, the self is something other, something that owns, uses and directs these aggregates?

In one of the poems of the early Buddhist saints there occur the following two stanzas:

> *Within this little five-doored hut an ape*
> *Doth prowl, and round and round from door to door*
> *He hies, rattling with blows again, again.*
>
> *Halt, ape! run thou not forth. For thee*
> *'Tis not herein as it was wont to be,*
> *Wisdom doth hold thee captive. Never more*
> *Shalt roam far hence (in freedom as of yore).*[2]

The five doors are clearly the five senses, the restless ape is the ego, but who is it that gives the order 'Halt, ape!'?

The Buddha's warning that none of the constituents of being is the self needs to be noted by surface-thinking Christians of the West. Many people tend to identify the body with the real person and at deathbeds or funerals

[1] Translation by E. J. Thomas, *The Quest of Enlightenment*, John Murray, 1950.   [2] *Thera-gātha* (PTS), 125–6.

57

think that the end of the body is the end of being, instead of thinking of the funeral as the disposal of out-worn physical 'clothing', the self continuing in a spiritual sphere. Similarly some people tend to think of their feelings as the essentially personal element, or the conscious mind as the self, or consciousness itself, whereas in some cases brain deterioration or damage prevents efficient or sane functioning. In sleep or in the grip of some diseases or injuries normal consciousness is no longer in operation and a sub-consciousness comes closer to the surface. This last point has a common relevance to Buddhist and modern psychology and will be considered in the next chapter.

In a section of the *Dhamma-pada* dealing with the self, the man who holds himself as dear is urged to watch the self carefully, if he is to teach others he is urged to carry out first what he teaches, he must keep himself well subdued.

Self is the lord of self, who else could be the lord? With self well subdued, a man finds a lord such as few can find.[1]

Evil is done by the self, holy living is achieved by the self.

Rouse thyself by thyself, examine thyself by thyself, thus self-protected and attentive wilt thou live happily, O monk. For self is the lord of self, self is the refuge of self; therefore curb thyself as the merchant curbs a noble horse.[2]

I have deliberately chosen one of the older translations in which the reflexive pronoun is used, but even here

[1] *Dhamma-pada*, 160.   [2] Ibid., 379–80.

there seems to be some entity which examines, subdues, and curbs, as if the man were over the self.

In the teaching of the Buddha there is certainly a self which needs to be recognized and repudiated, an ever-changing, superficial, grasping, possessive being, the stream of feelings, thoughts and desires, which insists on its own absolute individuality and independence. This is the self which is criticized and reproved in the Pitakas, and which can rightly be characterized as impermanent, without lasting self-hood or substance. Often this self is spoken of in modern terms as the ego.

The ego was, it seemed, endlessly immeshed in the move-ment of becoming, so much so that under a critical scrutiny it could appear to have no existence of its own, but to be a mere point of acquiescence in a succession of momentary impulses, feelings, thoughts and sensations. Yet there was something that persisted and that could, in some measure, quicken or retard the movement and, superficially at least, control or direct it. Did this capacity derive from a Self in the individual independent of the movement, a Principle of being which, though present in the world of becoming, was unattached to it and which, in becoming, did not cease infinitely to be and to know?[1]

But, as we have already seen, there is a sense in which the Buddha speaks of the self as good and dear. In a conversation with the King of Kosala, the Buddha does not in any way correct the King's remarks to the effect that evil conduct in thought, word and deed is treating

[1] l'Anson Fausset, *The Flame and the Light*, Abelard Schuman, p. 19.

the self as a foe, good conduct as a dear friend. He even
endorses the view

> *Since aye so dear the self to others is,*
> *Let the self-lover harm no other man.*

This is very close to the second great commandment of
Judaism and Christianity, 'Thou shalt love thy neighbour
as thyself', the true love of self is the measure by which
we should love others.

> *The whole wide world we traverse with our thought,*
> *finding to man naught dearer than the self;*
> *Since aye so dear the self to others is,*
> *let the self-lover harm no other man.*[1]

There seems, therefore, valid reason for thinking that
there are two kinds of self in the recorded sayings of the
Buddha, a lower self to be unmasked, tamed and repudiated, and a true Self to be loved and developed.
This Self is to be sought for, and when found made the
refuge and centre of a man's life.

There is in the *Vinaya*, the Book of Discipline for
monks, the incident of a party of young men who set
out with their wives for a picnic in a wood. One of them
having no wife brought with him instead a prostitute,
who at a quiet moment made off with some of their
property. The young men pursued her and coming
across the Buddha asked if he had seen her, to which
he replied 'What now, young men, do you think? Which
were the better to you? To go tracking the woman or to
go tracking yourselves?' When the pursuers replied

[1] *Udāna Sutta* (PTS), 47.

that it would be better to seek themselves, the Buddha invited them to sit down so that he might teach them Dhamma.

Another interesting incident is the visit to the Buddha of a certain wanderer named Vacchagotta, who wanted to know if there was an *ātman* or self. The Buddha was silent and finally his questioner went away. Later Ananda asks the Buddha why he was silent and receives the following explanation:

If I had answered "There is a self", that would be siding with those who hold the eternalist theory. . . . If I had answered 'There is no self', then that would be siding with those who hold the annihilationist theory. . . . If I had answered 'There is a self', would that be in accordance with my knowledge that all things are without self? . . . If I had answered 'There is no self', then that would have been a greater confusion to the already confused Vacchagotta. For he would have thought: Formerly indeed I had an *ātman* (self), but now I have not got one.[1]

The Buddha clearly thought that any direct answer would have been misunderstood and distorted by controversialists. Possibly he felt himself in a similar position to Jesus who 'knows that the moment he says "Messiah" he will be drawn into a network of illusions, so he remains silent and tries first to convert their hearts'.

The question of 'Who am I?' or perhaps better 'Who is I?' is a vital one; it is the main discussion between Christianity and Buddhism, so vital that no quarter can

[1] Summarized from Rahula, op. cit., p. 63.

be asked or given. Extreme Theravada Buddhists hold that there is no self, but only a superficial, ever-changing, restless stream of feelings, thoughts and desires. Christians would agree that the ever-changing, ever-grasping thing that most people call 'self' is not the true self, but that right down in the very depths of being there is a deep entity, which passes judgement on the ego or empirical self, which controls and uses body and mind, which survives death, and which is akin to whatever is the mover of the Universe.

If there is such a true self, it would be very difficult to describe it:

Suppose that I am trying to make a scientific study of myself. I shall, of course, have to ask myself questions, making experiments on myself to test my reactions to this or that stimulus. When I have made the experiments and asked the questions, some part of me must receive the answers and draw correct conclusions from them. If it is the 'I' who is asking the questions, then there must always be a bit of myself – the bit that does the asking – which I cannot examine. A large part of myself may be the 'examinee', but there must always be a bit left over to be the 'examiner'. Science can be used to describe the first of these, but it cannot describe the second. Or, more precisely, it can only describe it in the past, never in the present. As Herbert Dingle has said, there is a 'non-objectivizable I' of whom I have immediate knowledge, different in character from my knowledge of anything else. To say that it is non-objectivizable is to say that I cannot talk about it, for immediately I do so it becomes the object of my speech and is no longer 'I' but 'me'.[1]

[1] C. A. Coulson, *Science and Christian Belief*, OUP, 1955 (Fontana Books, 1958, p. 118).

The Doctrine of Non-Self

This thought from an avowedly Christian writer is paralleled by another Western writer, who has found the study of Eastern thought an engrossing spiritual adventure, bringing new meaning and inward enrichment to life:

We can observe and study objectively the changing complex of thought and mood, which we miscall self. But what we are and are not, the *Atman*, the 'Suchness', we can never observe, because It is Its own object and, as such, mediates unseen, though not unfelt or unknown inwardly, between subject and object, in us and in all else, as a reconciling principle.[1]

If this clue from Coulson and l'Anson Fausset is a right one, the Buddha was silent, not because he thought there was no self, but because the true self cannot be described but only experienced. It is something too ineffable for words. As he lay dying he charged his disciples:

Therefore, Ananda, dwell making yourselves your island, making yourselves, not anyone else, your refuge; making the Dhamma your island, the Dhamma your refuge, nothing else your refuge.

Here Dhamma and self seem to be equated. Dhamma is regarded as transcendent and eternal. Must not self be of the same nature? The two are linked together in another word attributed to the Buddha:

There is not in the world an evil deed that does lie hid.
The Self, O man, knows what of thee is true or false.

[1] l'Anson Fausset, op. cit., pp. 176f.

63

Ah sir, the lovely Self, the witness, thou dost despise
Who in the self hideth the self that is evil.
Devas and Truth-finders see the fool walking unevenly in the
*   world; ,*
Wherefore let the 'master of himself' walk recollectedly,
The 'master of the worlds' heedfully, contemplative,
The 'master of Dhamma', dhamma-farer, fails not (of the
*   goal).*[1]

Christmas Humphreys, who has the courage to retain what he thinks to be true in the Christian tradition and to criticize what he thinks to be mistaken in the Buddhist interpretation of life, is outspoken in his rejection of the extreme Theravāda position:

All things, without exception, said the Buddha, are *anicca*, changing; live accordingly. All things, seen and unseen, are *anatta*, without a separate self. I have, since I first read of this doctrine at the age of seventeen, entirely rejected the modern concept of its meaning as an unqualified no-self, partly because the Buddha, according to the Pali Canon, taught nothing of the kind; partly because, as I read it, he taught by his silence and in other ways precisely the opposite, and mostly because I reject a statement of fact which every faculty of knowledge I possess, including the intuition, informs me to be quite untrue. On the other hand, I entirely accept the doctrine that there is not in me, nor in any man, a single faculty or part which is unchangingly mine or his, or eternal, or separate from that All which men call variously the Dharma-kaya or Buddha-nature or Reality or God. This is a doctrine of enormous value to all men and I believe that the Buddha taught it.[2]

[1] *Anguttara-Nikāya* (PTS), i, 147–150.
[2] Christmas Humphreys, *Studies in the Middle Way*, Luzac, 1948, pp. 148f.

6

Experiencing the Self

>>> ✦ <<<

BUDDHISM is a religion which emphasizes deeds rather than creeds. It is more a way of life than a summary of beliefs. It stresses the connection between cause and effect, and urges men to do actions in the present which will produce good results in the future, either in this life or in succeeding lives. 'Experience' and 'action' are its keywords. It is therefore true to the spirit of Buddhism for man to examine carefully his own experience in the hope of gaining some light about this central question of the self. Can man experience or feel the self?

The psychologist Jung in his practice of depth psychology seems to have discovered the existence of an immortal soul or self in man. He speaks of three levels within the life of man: the level of consciousness, thoughts and feelings and memories, at the centre of which is the ego which believes itself to be in control of the whole of a man's life, and likes to regard itself as autonomous. Secondly there is the personal unconscious, in which is stored up all that we cannot or do not want to remember as well as a content of innate possibilities and energies. Some idea of what goes on in this sub-conscious level can be gained by a study of dreams and of the irrational impulses which express themselves in conscious life

E   65

from time to time. Thirdly there is the collective unconscious, common to all men and indeed to all life,
deeper than individual personality and prior to it, which
contains materials collectively held by all men. X

Man's life on all three levels must be recognized and
harmonized. Hindus and Buddhists are critical of the
failure of so many Christians to recognize some kind of
identity with the whole of nature. If they were speaking
in Christian terms they would say that we fail to see
ourselves as part of God's creation, that the same
creative force is at work in ourselves as in animal and
vegetable life, that we are not independent and autonomous. Jung says much the same thing:

Jung's concept of self is not that of a kind of universal
consciousness which is really only another name for the
unconscious. It consists rather on the one hand in the awareness of our unique natures, and on the other of our intimate
relationship with all life, not only human, but animal and
plant, even that of inorganic nature and the cosmos itself.
It brings a feeling of oneness and reconciliation with life,
which can now be accepted as it is, not as it ought to be.[1]

Most men live at the level of the ego, with occasional
unaccountable uprushes from the unconscious. The
mature man seeks to unify or integrate these two levels,
when a new centre of personality will emerge, differing
in nature from the ego-centre. Jung calls this resulting
new centre of personality 'the self'.

[1] Frieda Fordham, *Introduction to Jung's Psychology*, Penguin,
1953, p. 63.

Experiencing the Self

Through the practice of depth psychology Jung has done in the twentieth century A.D. what the Hindus did perhaps in the eighth century B.C.; he has discovered empirically the existence of an immortal soul in man, dwelling outside time and space, which can actually be experienced. This soul Jung, like the Hindus, calls the 'self'; and the concept of the 'self' is central to his psychology and gives it religious content. By the self he does not mean the 'ego', the ordinary experiencing agent, or the conscious mind; he means something altogether different and extremely difficult to describe in words. . . . Most basically it is the entity in man which reconciles the opposites in the psyche and which transcends time and space.[1]

Within the collective unconscious operate archetypes which are the psychological counterparts of instincts, forms of apprehension which exist before consciousness, conditions of intuition with which we are born. Just as the instincts make us behave in a human way, so the archetypes make us express our thinking and feeling, conscious and unconscious, in human forms. Thus we all tend to express our experience in similar symbols and images.

Jung holds that there is in the unconscious an archetype of wholeness, something within trying to harmonize the conscious and the unconscious. This urge to wholeness is independent of the conscious will, and according to Jung occupies a central position which approximates to the God-image in the unconscious of religious people. Yet like the Buddha he will not go beyond human

[1] R. C. Zaehner, *The Concise Encylopaedia of Living Faiths*, Hutchinson, 1959, p. 403.

experience, and so he speaks of the God-image *in* man only, and does not proceed to relate it with the transcendent God of the prophetic religions. Nor does he deny this identity or relationship.✗The idea of God is a psychological fact; the essential being of God is something lying outside human experience, and therefore to Jung unverifiable, as to the Buddha. What we have gained from Jung to help us in the Buddhist-Christian dialogue is his recognition that there is a self which can be experienced.

Indeed Jungian psychology sees the goal of life as the bringing of the self, 'that eternal substance', 'which lives in the everlasting now', right up into consciousness, and in integrating this 'divine child' both with consciousness and with our ordinary world of space and time. Jung himself watched this process happening in scores of patients, amounting to the growth of a new centre of personality, achieving a new sense of wholeness. He calls this process individuation or integration.

William James in an earlier generation to Jung came to a similar conclusion. He formulated his thinking under four heads; the first two of which anticipated Jung, and the second two, go further than Jung in a Christian direction:

1. 'there is something wrong about us as we naturally stand',
2. this leads to the discovery of 'the germinal higher part' in a man,
3. this germinal higher part is conterminous and continues with a MORE of like quality,

4. from the contact with a MORE by way of the
   germinal higher part the 'real being' forms.[1]

Christians would say that man is made in the image
of God and that this divine kinship lies hidden in the
depths of personality or self or spirit. It must be sought
and recognized and allowed to take over control of the
conscious life and leadership in the affairs of life. Before
this can be done, however, the Christian needs to
recognize the existence of a usurping self, 'the old man',
the lower self, which has to be killed off before 'the new
man', the true self can come into its own. This corres-
ponds to the self which Buddhism calls men to repudiate,
that kaleidoscopic succession of thoughts and feelings,
desires and graspings, in which there is no permanent
and true selfhood.

Jesus made this self-noughting a condition of discipleship:

If any man would come after me, let him deny himself, and
take up his cross, and follow me.[2]

The self-denial demanded was not the anaemic forms
of abstinence which some Christians adopt in Lent, but
a thorough-going repudiation of the old self, a costly
self-noughting, a mortification. The point of taking up
a cross was to carry it to the place of execution and be
crucified on it. Before the new man can be born, the
old man must be crucified; before the true self can come
into being, the selfish ego must die. Psychologically, the

---

[1] As summarized by P. W. Martin, *Experiment in Depth*, Routledge
and Kegan Paul, 1955, p. 199.　　　　　　　　　[2] Mark 8.34.

work of the Buddha must be accomplished within the being of man, before the Christ can begin to do his work. Christ, recognized or unrecognized, carries on where the Buddha left off.

I have been crucified with Christ; yet I live; and yet no longer I, but Christ liveth in me: and that life which I now live in the flesh I live in faith, the faith which is in the Son of God, who loved me, and gave himself up for me.[1]

When the unconscious self has been recognized and allowed to operate, it brings intuitive wisdom and un-expected power to the integrated personality.

My psychological experience has shown time and time again that certain contents issue from a psyche more complete than consciousness. They often contain a superior analysis or insight or knowledge which consciousness has not been able to produce. We have a suitable word for such occurrences – intuition. In pronouncing it most people have an agreeable feeling as if something had been settled. But they never take into account that you do not *make* an intuition. On the contrary it always comes to you; you *have* a hunch, it has produced itself and you only catch it if you are clever or quick enough.[2]

Here Buddhism and Jungian psychology are in agreement once again, for intuition is the key word of Zen Buddhism, which aims at transcending intellectual thought and gaining direct touch with reality. Sekiso, an early Zen master urging a discipline in which perfect motionlessness and unawareness are attained, continues.

[1] Gal. 2.20.
[2] C. G. Jung, *Psychology and Religion*, Yale, 1938, p. 49.

Experiencing the Self

All the signs of life will depart and also every trace of limitation will vanish. Not a single idea will disturb your consciousness, when lo! all of a sudden you will come to realize a light abounding in full gladness. It is like coming across a light in thick darkness; it is like receiving treasure in poverty. The four elements and the five aggregates are no more felt as burdens; so light, so easy, so free you are. Your very existence has been delivered from all limitations; you have become open, light, and transparent. You gain an illuminating insight into the very nature of things, which now appear to you as so many fairylike flowers having no graspable realities. Here is manifested the unsophisticated self which is the original face of your being; here is shown all bare the most beautiful landscape of your birthplace. There is but one straight passage open and unobstructed through and through. This is so when you surrender all – your body, your life, and all that belongs to your inmost self. This is where you gain peace, ease, non-doing, and inexpressible delight. . . . It is like unlocking the door to a treasury; when the entrance is once gained, every object coming into your view is yours, every opportunity that presents itself is available for your use.[1]

Asked where these intuitions come from, most Zen Buddhists would probably answer that they come from the deep self, some would say that they come from the Buddha-heart within man's being. Christians would want to discuss with Buddhists and others their own interpretation that such intuitions may come from God, arising from the image of God within, which makes men potential 'partakers of the divine nature'.

[1] Quoted in D. T. Suzuki, *Introduction to Zen Buddhism* (Arrow Books), Rider, 1949, p. 46.

The quotation from Sekiso makes clear a belief in the self as 'the original face of your being'. It also emphasizes the blessing, joy and peace that come from this experience of the self, of which Jung says:

It is as if a river that had run to waste in sluggish sidestreams suddenly found its way back to its proper bed, or as if a stone lying on a germinating seed were lifted away so that the shoot could begin its natural growth.[1]

'Take away the stone' of the old self, and the new self, the true self can come forth out of the tomb where it has lain hidden so long. St Paul again confirms this experience:

If any man is in Christ, there is a new creation: the old things are passed away: behold, they are become new.[2]

Meister Eckhart with whom Suzuki finds many points of contact, speaks of the difficulty of describing this inmost self:

There is a spirit in the soul, untouched by time and flesh, flowing from the spirit, remaining in the spirit, itself wholly spiritual. In this principle is God, ever verdant, ever flowing in all the joy and glory of his actual Self. Sometimes I have called that principle the Tabernacle of the soul, sometimes a spiritual Light, anon I say it is a Spark. But now I say it is more exalted over this and that than the heavens are exalted above the earth. So now I name it in a nobler fashion. . . . It is free of all names, and void of all forms. It is one and simple as God is one and simple, and no man can in any wise behold it.[3]

[1] C. G. Jung, *The Development of Personality*, Routledge and Kegan Paul, 1954, p. 184.   [2] II Cor. 5.17, RV, mg.
[3] Quoted by P. W. Martin, *Experiment in Depth*, p. 133.

72

Experiencing the Self

This self, then, cannot be described, it can only be experienced. A man may only say 'I am': he cannot describe this self as an object, for he is the experiencing subject. The Christian believes, however, that he is akin to God, made in the image of God. Yet, as Jung laments, 'too few people have experienced the divine image as the innermost possession of their own souls. Christ only meets them from without, never from within the soul'.[1]

It is the image of God in man that makes him capable of response to God when God comes to him from outside, or indeed when God moves within the being of man. Jesus was the coming of God to men in order that they might discover that there was something divine in men already. It is that image of God in man that enables him to recognize God when he comes in Christ. H. G. Wood quotes the story of an old Hindu, who, having heard one sermon on the life of Christ, asked to be baptized. 'How can you ask for this?' asked the missionary, 'have you ever heard before today the name of Jesus Christ?' 'No,' replied the old man, 'but I have known and sought him all my life.'

The Christian recognizes Christ as God's light in every man's heart: 'There was the true light which lighteth every man coming into the world.'[2] When he comes to them from without, men can recognize him from within. 'Behold, I stand at the door and knock,' says the living Christ in the vision of the Book of Revelation, 'if any man hear my voice and open the door, I will come in to

[1] C. G. Jung, *Psychology and Alchemy* (Collected Works, Vol. 12), Routledge and Kegan Paul, 1953, p. 12.   [2] John 1.9.

73

him, and will sup with him, and he with me.'[1] The knock from without is meant to awaken the true self, the image of God within, which will then recognize the divine visitor and invite him in. Then it will be possible to say, 'Today is salvation come to this house' – in the conscious communion of God with man-made-in-the-image-of-God, in the voluntary identification of the human will with the divine will, and in the outpouring of divine life from the Creator to his beloved creature.

The Holy Spirit is God in man, the Spirit of Jesus come to be in men, as a guest, not to annihilate or absorb man's personality, but to help the seed of the divine image to germinate and grow, 'till we all attain . . . unto a full-grown man, unto the measure of the stature of the fulness of Christ'.[2] With the Holy Spirit within the human spirit, the true self, there will be wholeness and unity, growing sanctification, increasingly selfless love, perception of truth, a degree of inspiration or intuition that transcends cerebral thinking and a peace that the world cannot give and cannot take away. In this context the sevenfold gift of the Spirit comes alive with meaning – the spirit of wisdom and understanding, the spirit of counsel and spiritual strength, the spirit of knowledge and true godliness, and the spirit of holy fear.

In their encounter with Buddhists Christians have to show a radical degree of self-noughting, they must be conscious of the image of God within, allow it to grow and integrate the whole of life, and by constant com-

[1] Rev. 3.20.   [2] Eph. 4.13.

munion with God draw from him the spiritual life necessary to do this. Only in that way will they be able to bear convincing witness to the existence of a true self and a true God. The Buddhist, as always, will judge by results and not by beliefs or claims.

The appeal to experience should be addressed to Christians in a further way, namely in the study of the life of prayer and meditation and of the lives of the mystics. In the new encounter which is taking place between religions, the experience of the mystics and men of prayer of all religions affords common ground for exploration. In this deeper encounter the religious communities of the Christian Church have an important part to play, and so have the Christian Ashrams which live on a more Eastern pattern. A Christian community of monks living according to Buddhist rule in a Buddhist country would gain valuable insights, and it would be interesting to compare their experience with that of the Buddhist Vihara of English and Asian monks in West London, which is trying to adapt the Buddhist practice of the spiritual life to Western conditions.

7

The Cause of Pain

>>> ✧ <<<

Wʜᴀᴛ is the Noble Truth of the cause of pain? It is craving
tending to rebirth, combined with delight and passion, and
finding delight here and there. This, monks, is the Noble
Truth of the cause of pain.[1]

Here the Buddha has identified the cause of *dukkha*,
man's pain of heart and mind, his sense of discord,
meaninglessness, impermanence and imperfection. It
is craving, attachment to the passions of the body and
the things of the world, the wrong conclusion that final
blessedness consists in the continuation of the here and
now, the prolongation of this life. The result is that man
is chained to this pain, because he is bent on eternalizing
what he mistakenly thinks to be the self, and in consequence he refuses the travail of change. His ever-
changing self is constantly being reborn much the same
as before, instead of accepting the death of the only self
he knows in order that the true self may come to life.

One night the Buddha and his disciples were watching
from afar a forest fire, which afforded an initial illustra-
tion for teaching which has ever since been known as the
Fire Sermon:

[1] Translation by E. J. Thomas, *The Quest of Enlightenment*.

The Cause of Pain

For everything, he declared, O monks, is in flames. And what everything is in flames? The eye is in flames. The visible is in flames, the knowledge of the visible is in flames; the feeling which arises from contact with the visible, be it pleasure, be it pain, be it neither pleasure nor pain, this also is in flames. By what fire is it kindled? by the fire of desire, by the fire of hate, by the fire of fascination, it is kindled; by birth, old age, death, pain, lamentation, sorrow, grief, distress, it is kindled. . . .

Knowing this, O monks, one who is wise becomes weary of the eye, he becomes weary of the visible, he becomes weary of the feeling which arises from contact with the visible, be it pleasure, be it pain, be it neither pleasure nor pain.[1]

There is here both recognition of the fires of desire, hate and delusion, and also the disillusionment that follows their recognition. Had the Buddha gone no further, he would have indeed uttered a vivid warning, but he would have been as pessimistic as the writer of Ecclesiastes. He, however, faces the diagnosis of man's condition, courageously and relentlessly, and in the third and fourth Noble Truths will go on to prescribe the cure. For the Buddha is above everything else an exponent of the law of causality: every happening has an earlier cause, every present deed will have a consequent effect:

I will teach you *dhamma*: IF THIS IS, THAT COMES TO BE; from the arising of this, that arises: if this is not, that does not come to be; from the ceasing of this, that ceases.[2]

[1] Quoted from l'Anson Fausset, *The Flame and the Light*.
[2] *Majjhima-Nikāya* (PTS), ii, 32.

The *Dhamma-pada*, that early collection of Gautama's sayings opens with these twin-verses:

All that we are is the result of what we have thought: it is founded on our thoughts, it is made up of our thoughts. If a man speaks or acts with an evil thought, pain follows him, as the wheel follows the foot of the ox that draws the cart. . . . If a man speaks or acts with a pure thought, happiness follows him, like a shadow that never leaves him.[1]

This principle of happening and cause in its backward looking sense, of cause and effect in its forward look, is the Law of Karma. The word *Karma* means action or doing, and the Law of Karma is the theory of cause and effect, the logical consequence of deeds. Good actions produce good results, bad actions produce bad results. Christians often fail to understand the Law of Karma, because they try to read into it the ideas of moral justice and of reward and punishment, arising from belief in a supreme being, who is both Law Giver and Judge. To Buddhists the Law of Karma is a natural law, knowledge of which can be creative of the future, as it has been productive of the present.

The twin-verses of the *Dhamma-pada*, quoted above, emphasize the initial importance of thought, as producing the bad or good words or action. Other passages in the *Pitakas* (scriptures) emphasize this and that still prior factor of will in the thinker, speaker and doer:

It is the custom for a Truth-finder (*Tathāgata*) to lay down 'Deed, deed'. I lay down three kinds of deeds for the doing of an evil deed: deed of body, deed of speech, deed of mind.

[1] *Dhamma-pada* 1 and 2.

The Cause of Pain

Of these three kinds of deeds thus classified, I lay down that
a deed of mind is the most greatly censurable in the doing
of an evil deed.[1]

I, monks, say that willing is a deed. Having willed, one
does a deed, through body, speech or thought. . . . The fruit
of a deed is threefold: it may arise here and now, or later,
or in a succession of lives.[2]

The Buddha thus emphasized the originating and
creative quality of will; he called to men to create their
own future by willing and doing right deeds now, and
his earliest followers are described by Mrs Rhys Davids
as 'will-missioners'. 'Work out your own salvation with
diligence' crystallized his message. This life and succeeding lives were the opportunity of 'making-to-become';
men were to be creative workers for their own salvation.

The Buddhist would note with welcome that the New
Testament has its emphasis on the harvest of deeds:

Be not deceived; God is not mocked: for whatsoever a man
soweth, that shall he also reap. For he that soweth unto his
own flesh shall of the flesh reap corruption; but he that
soweth unto the Spirit shall of the Spirit reap eternal life.
And let us not be weary in well-doing: for in due season we
shall reap, if we faint not. So then, as we have opportunity,
let us work that which is good toward all men.[3]

Buddhists emphasize the law, Christians the law-giver.
Both insist on the principle. In popular thinking Buddhists
tend to interpret the Law of Karma as referring more
to a man's present fate, his present happiness or mis-

[1] *Majjhima-Nikāya* (PTS), i, 373.
[2] *Anguttara-Nikāya*, iii, 415.   [3] Gal. 6.7–10.

fortune, almost in the sense of something for which he is not responsible, something beyond his control which has brought him to his present state. Christians could express more explicit agreement in the thought of the Law of Karma as operating in the production of character rather than in fate. On the first Good Friday, three men were hanging on crosses: their execution was the fruit of their deeds, but they had come there by different paths in the working of the Law of Karma. One of the two thieves brings this out in his reproof to the other:

Dost thou not even fear God, seeing thou art in the same condemnation? And we indeed justly: for we receive the due reward of our deeds: but this man hath done nothing amiss.[1]

The two thieves had come there as a result of a life of crime. Jesus had come there as a result of his obedience to God's will. His trust in God had built up an inner character which resulted in a willing acceptance of the cross and a refusal to fail in love. One of the two thieves continues in his rebellion against everything and everybody, and goes on in his darkness, into deeper darkness. His companion is moved by the bearing of Jesus and is delivered from final hopelessness and frustration by a new example and a new friendship. A new factor has come into his life which will have its result in the Kingdom of the dead. 'Today, shalt thou be with me in Paradise.'

The relationship of the Christian doctrine of forgiveness to this law of cause and effect needs to be made clear. Christians and Buddhists in encounter tend to

[1] Luke 23.40–41.

think that they are completely incompatible. The Buddhist thinks that forgiveness is an easy way out of responsibility for the past and that the Christian idea is of an easy-going God whose standard of justice is less than his standard of mercy. It seems to him a more honourable thing that a man should have to work off the consequences of his bad deeds in a succession of lives until the last farthing is paid. The Bible, however, speaks of the wrath of God, not as unreasoning, arbitrary and self-regarding anger, but as his unceasing and relentless opposition to all evil, because it is spoiling his children and the world he has created for them to live in. God loves men and is grieved at their sins, but his love has an inexorable quality about it, which will never let men go, never let them down in their need, and never be content with anything less than the perfection which is his will for them.

Yet in his love God comes to meet men, to restore the relationship which has been broken by men's sin, to stretch out the hand of reconciliation which man can only really take if he has altered his attitude to his sin. 'God was in Christ reconciling the world unto himself': man must be prepared to accept humbly and gratefully that reconciliation. The cost to God in human terms was the cross of Jesus: the cost to man is the travail of a new birth. Something new has taken place, the result of the restored relationship is that the love and power of God can pass from God to man to strengthen man's will to do good deeds and lead him forward on the road to holiness and blessing.

F

The final hell is to be abandoned to one's own character, all will gone and no new saving factor; similarly, the bliss of heaven is to be eternally established in holiness:

He that is unrighteous, let him do unrighteousness still: and he that is filthy, let him be made filthy still: and he that is righteous, let him do righteousness still: and he that is holy, let him be made holy still.[1]

The law is there, but the writer of the Book of Revelation sees the presence of the law-giver there also, to establish the law which he has planted in human nature:

Behold, I come quickly; and my reward is with me, to render to each man according as his work is. I am the Alpha and the Omega, the first and the last, the beginning and the end.[2]

According to Buddhism, the effect of an action may continue in life after death; desire, craving, greed, lust, attachment to the body and the world, attachment even to life itself cause rebirth in a succession of lives. They argue, and rightly, that 95 per cent of Buddhists and Christians alike are not fit to enter Nirvana or its equivalent; there must be a further sphere or spheres of education, enlightenment and progress. Their point seems justified when they find so many Christians holding that at death men are put into cold storage until the day of judgement, with no further opportunities of growth or deterioration.

[1] Rev. 22.11.   [2] Rev. 22.12.

The Cause of Pain

But to continue with the arguments for rebirth. Buddhists mention that peculiar feeling that we all get from time to time of having been in a place before or about to take part in an action which seems to be familiar. They explain love at first sight as due to the lovers having loved one another in a previous existence; and infant prodigies as due to knowledge or skill acquired in some previous life. Dreams are explained as being memories from past lives, rather than the activity of the unconscious self concerning itself with the problems of this life. In Burma one was often told of children, who at the age of five or six could remember their past existences, though the memory soon faded. In the years following the death of a Dalai Lama in Tibet, search begins for a child born at that time or even after, and a variety of things are put before him. If he unerringly chooses those belonging to the previous Dalai Lama it is regarded as proof that he is a reincarnation.

Buddhists today are no longer content to quote Buddhist evidence only, they produce arguments from the New Testament, such as the words of Jesus about John the Baptist 'This is Elijah which is to come' or the reply of the disciples to his question about men's opinions of himself, 'Some say John the Baptist, some Elijah: and others Jeremiah or one of the prophets.' In St John's Gospel Jesus is asked, 'Rabbi, who did sin, this man or his parents that he should be born blind?'[1] A Christian writer, Leslie Weatherhead, commenting on this verse, says:

[1] John 9.2.

83

If it were contemplated that a man *born* blind was being punished by blindness for sin committed, then that sin committed must have been in an earlier life before he was born into this world.

Yet the most that can be said is that in the time of Jesus reincarnation was a current idea. It cannot be deduced from the New Testament, nor, on the other hand, is it explicitly denied. There is, however, one text in the Epistle of James which has a Buddhist note about it:

The tongue is a fire: the world of iniquity among our members is the tongue, which defileth the whole body, and setteth on fire the wheel of birth, and is set on fire by hell.[1]

'The wheel of birth' signifies endless repetition without progress.

More obvious reference can be seen in a number of English poets including Wordsworth, Tennyson and Dante Gabriel Rossetti; one quotation must suffice, from John Masefield:

> *I hold that when a person dies,*
> *His soul returns again to earth;*
> *Arrayed in some new flesh-disguise*
> *Another mother gives him birth.*
> *With sturdier limbs and brighter brain*
> *The old soul takes the road again.[2]*

The most powerful argument against successive re-births is the lack of conscious continuity between them.

[1] James 3.6, RV, mg.
[2] John Masefield, 'The Creed', in *Collected Poems*.

The Cause of Pain

If there is no memory of deeds done in a past life can the person in question be held responsible for them? Certainly, it was claimed of the Buddha that on the night of his enlightenment he saw and understood all his past lives. According to Buddhism every man can become a Buddha, and it might be argued that when each attains to this enlightenment the whole of his past may be seen in perspective and meaning.

Christians would agree with Buddhists that every man needs a new birth. Jesus in his conversation with Nicodemus said that unless a man be born again, he will neither see nor enter the Kingdom of Heaven. It is a new beginning that is demanded, where the past has been recognized for what it is, where the old self has died and the new self brought to life. He must be born again and grow up in the new life as simple and trusting as a child, not claiming autonomy, nor grasping at everything within reach, but dependent on God his Father and full of wonder at the world and life in it, yet not attached to the world, ever moving forward to eternal life.

Until this radical new birth takes place man does not recognize or live by his true and permanent self. He is just a stream of thoughts, feelings, desires and consciousness, a succession of disconnected moments with no thread of continuity. But when he comes to himself, he recognizes the impermanence and unreality of what he used to think of as himself, he also recognizes the reality of something new, deep down within himself, no longer the shuttlecock of circumstances, but the unshaken victor in them, the controller of feelings and thoughts, the director of consciousness. A man who has not experienced this in this life, will have to do so in the future life. At the moment of death, we all start in the next life from what the Buddhist would call the Karmic level and what the Christian would think of as the level of character he has attained in this life.

One sometimes wonders if the truth which Buddhists are feeling after in their belief in recurring births is that until a man has found his true and permanent self, he is nothing more than a series of momentary selves or moments of consciousness, which are like the series of static photographs which make up a film. The human eye cannot perceive distinctly and separately photographs which succeed one another at a speed greater than one-tenth of a second; yet when shown through a projector the successive photographs seem to be a succession of movement. In the same way, thoughts and feelings flit one after another through a man's consciousness and seem continuous, but until given a connecting thread, through the action and control of the self, are merely disconnected moments. Is it possible that this can only be made clear to simple folk by the parables of reincarnation, stories of disconnected moments pictured as lives, working on the principle of the parable that truth embodied in a tale can enter very lowly doors?

8

The Stopping of Pain

>>> ✧ <<<

Wнат is the Noble Truth of the cessation of pain? It is the
complete and trackless destruction, cessation, abandonment,
relinquishment and rejection of that craving which tends to
rebirth and finds delight here and there. This, monks, is the
Noble Truth of the cessation of pain.[1]

In the first of the Noble Truths the Buddha described
the meaninglessness, impermanence, lack of abiding
reality in life as it is lived by the great majority of
people, the pain of heart and mind as well as the sufferings and misfortunes which are the common lot. In the
second truth he identified the cause as craving or desire
or thirst which leads to a continuation of the very
existence from which men are trying to escape. The third
Truth is a very simple prescription for cure – destroy,
stop, abandon, relinquish and reject the root cause.

The complete cessation of *dukkha*, pain, is Nirvana.
This is a difficult term to define, for the Buddha, while
urging it upon his followers as the goal of all effort,
declined to say much about it: 'If you ask what Nirvana
is for – this question goes too far, and is beyond the
compass of an answer.'

The difficulty of describing Nirvana, but the reality

[1] Translation by E. J. Thomas, *The Quest of Enlightenment.*

of it, is well illustrated in a conversation between King Milinda of Ceylon and the monk Nagasena:

'But what, revered sir, is that Nirvana like that can be illustrated by similes? Convince me with reasons according to which a thing that is can be illustrated by similes.'

'Is there, sire, what is called wind?'

'Yes, revered sir.'

'Please, sire, show the wind by its colour or configuration or as thin or thick or long or short.'

But it is not possible, revered Nagasena, for the wind to be shown; for the wind cannot be grasped in the hand or touched; but yet there is the wind.'

'If, sire, it is not possible for the wind to be shown, well then, there is no wind.'

'I, revered Nagasena, know that there is wind, I am convinced of it, but I am not able to show the wind.'

'Even so, sire, there is Nirvana; but it is not possible to show Nirvana by colour or configuration.'

'Very good, revered Nagasena, well shown is the simile, well seen the reason; thus it is and I accept it as you say: There is Nirvana.'[1]

Dr Radhakrishnan emphasizes the ineffable nature of Nirvana:

The Buddha's real attitude is probably that Nirvana is a state of perfection inconceivable by us, and that if we are obliged to to offer descriptions of it, it is best to bring out its inconceivability by negative descriptions, its richness of content by positive predicates, realizing all the time that such descriptions are at best approximations only.[2]

[1] *The Questions of Milinda*, quoted from *Buddhist Texts* (E. Cassirer), pp. 99f.

[2] S. Radhakrishnan, *Indian Philosophy*, Allen and Unwin, 1929, p. 453.

The Stopping of Pain

The fact that Nirvana is usually described in negative terms has led some Western writers to think of it as completely negative, expressing annihilation or nothingness. The word itself means 'blown out', 'become cool', 'extinct': these meanings are not attached to Nirvana itself, but to the *arahant* (saint) who has reached Nirvana. The fires of desire, hatred and illusion have been extinguished; the heat of desire has become cool; he who has attained Nirvana will no longer be subject to rebirth, his wanderings have finished. In one sense, perhaps, Nirvana might be called annihilation, in that it is the annihilation of the false idea of self; indeed, the strict Buddhists of the Theravada tradition, that followed in Burma, Ceylon and Siam, would say that there is no other self, but, as we have seen, that is a debatable point, and one which cannot be proved from the scriptures. Possibly the conception of Nirvana as annihilation, which is held by some Buddhists, developed to fit in with the extreme *An-atta* doctrine of no-self, or it may have been the converse.

In the scriptures Nirvana is described as freedom, as deathless, the perfect purity, as other-worldly, as incomparable, as unconditioned, as the highest refuge, as peace and security. It is the complete opposite of *dukkha* (pain) with its characteristics of impermanence and lack of reality. Nirvana is the Ultimate in Buddhism, it is the Eternal.

There is, monks, an unborn, not become, not made, uncompounded, and were it not, monks, for this unborn, not become not made, uncompounded, no escape could be shown here, for what is born, has become, is made, is compounded. But because there is, monks, an unborn, not become, not made, uncompounded, therefore an escape can be shown for what is born, has become, is made, is compounded.[1]

The Commentary on the *Udāna Sutta* in which this passage occurs, interprets 'uncompounded' as 'unconstructed' or 'unconditioned', suggesting something standing in its own right and not dependent on any prior cause. Christians will note the similarity in language to the Athanasian Creed which describes the Godhead as uncreated, infinite, and eternal. The ultimate or highest concept in Buddhism is Nirvana; in Christianity as in Judaism and Islam, it is God.

Nirvana is also described in the scriptures as 'the stopping of becoming'. This could be interpreted merely as the stopping of rebirth; equally it might be explained as the end of all change and growth, because perfection has now been reached, becoming has found its goal in being. Nirvana is thus the goal of all Buddhist striving, it is the perfection of being, the highest blessing, the incomprehensible peace. In some of the *Psalms of the Brethren* and *Psalms of the Sisters*, the poems of the earliest monks and nuns, Nirvana is looked forward to with deep joy and radiant hope.

> *The escape therefrom, 'tis real, beyond the sphere*
> *Of reason, lasting, unborn, unproduced,*
> *The sorrowless, the stainless path that ends*
> *The things of woe, the peace from worries – bliss!*[2]

[1] *Udāna Sutta* (PTS), 80.   [2] *Psalms of the Sisters* (PTS).

90

The Stopping of Pain

Nirvana can be attained here and now in this world. It was so attained by Gautama, who after his enlightenment could have entered into its final blessedness, but delayed doing so for the sake of men. Walpole Rahula, a Buddhist monk of Ceylon, who has been quoted several times already, has an excellent description of the man who has already attained it, though it must be noted again that he insists that there is no self, only a false illusion of it:

He who has realized the Truth, Nirvana, is the happiest being in the world. He is free from all 'complexes' and obsessions, the worries and troubles that torment others. His mental health is perfect. He does not repent the past, nor does he brood over the future. He lives fully in the present. Therefore he appreciates and enjoys things in the purest sense without self-projections. He is joyful, exultant, enjoying the pure life, his faculties pleased, free from anxiety, serene and peaceful. As he is free from selfish desire, hatred, ignorance, conceit, pride, and all such 'defilements', he is pure and gentle, full of universal love, compassion, kindness, sympathy, understanding and tolerance. His service to others is of the purest, for he has no thought of self. He gains nothing, accumulates nothing, not even anything spiritual, because he is free from the illusion of Self, and the 'thirst' for becoming.[1]

There is clearly a longing in the heart of the Buddhist for the real, the perfect, the eternal, and a conviction that it cannot be found in the conditions of this life but must be sought elsewhere. A similar pilgrimage in search of the eternal is associated with Abraham and the patriarchs in the New Testament:

[1] Rahula, *What the Buddha Taught*, Gordon Fraser, p. 43.

By faith he [Abraham] became a sojourner in the land of promise, as in a land not his own, dwelling in tents, with Isaac and Jacob, the heirs with him of the same promise: for he looked for the city which hath the foundations, whose builder and maker is God. . . .

These all died in faith, not having received the promises, but having seen them and greeted them from afar, and having confessed that they were strangers and pilgrims on the earth. For they that say such things make it manifest that they are seeking after a country of their own. And if indeed they had been mindful of that country from which they went out, they would have had opportunity to return. But now they desire a better country, that is, a heavenly: wherefore God is not ashamed of them, to be called their God: for he hath prepared for them a city.[1]

The writer of the Epistle to the Hebrews speaks in a later chapter of this city as the goal and home of the human spirit, in which will be found innumerable hosts of angels, the general assembly and the church of the firstborn who are enrolled in heaven, and the spirits of just men made perfect. But to him it is above all the city of the living God, the Judge of all. So once again he warns us not to look for the permanent, the real and the unchanging in this world:

For we have not here an abiding city, but we seek after a city which is to come . . . a kingdom that cannot be shaken.[2]

The Book of Ecclesiastes gives us another clue to man's search for the lasting and real:

He [God] hath made everything beautiful in its time: also he hath set eternity in their heart, yet so that man cannot

[1] Heb. 11.9–10, 13–16.   [2] Heb. 13.14 and 12.28.

find out the work that God hath done from the beginning even to the end.[1]

If this alternative reading is the right one, the writer's thought is that there is something implanted in man by God, that makes him restless and unsatisfied, things beyond his understanding of which he is always in search of explanation. The writer's own disillusionment with life is a sign of this inner unrest. He is feeling after a truth made explicit centuries later when Augustine of Hippo, equally disillusioned with the pleasures of the world, diagnosed his own condition in the words, 'Thou hast made us for thyself, and our hearts shall find no rest until they find their rest in thee'.

The Buddha spoke of four stages on this long journey through the worlds to Nirvana. There is

the *Sotāpanna*, the Stream-Entrant, the one who has got into the stream, who has started toward the further shore of Nirvana;

the *Sakadāgāmi*, the Once Returner, who will come back once more among Gods or men;

the *Anāgāmi*, the Never Returner, who will never return to this life;

the *Arahant*, one who has reached the highest stage, the perfect one, completely liberated and full of wisdom.

The mention of Nirvana as the further shore and of the initiate who has started on the journey by getting into the stream, has a parallel in baptism, which is the Christian ceremony of initiation. There the Christian

[1] Eccles. 3.11, RV, mg.

literally goes down into the water, the waters close over his head to signify that the old man is dead, when he comes from the water it is as a new man, he is even given a new name. Those who are present pray that 'the old Adam in him may be so buried that the new man may be raised up in him', and 'that all evil desires of the flesh may die in him and all things belonging to the Spirit may live and grow in him'. It is recognized that the journey to the further shore is a perilous one so priest and people pray that 'he may so pass the waves of this troublesome world, that finally he may come to the land of eternal life'. One elaboration which the Church in Buddhist lands might well consider is that the first promise should renounce more explicitly the old, false self, as well as the devil and all his works, the world with all its empty attractions and the sinful desires of the flesh. Baptism could be a most meaningful experience to the Buddhist.

9

Magga: The Way

>>> ✧ <<<

THIS noble eightfold way itself is for the realization of Nirvana, that is to say right view, right thought, right speech, right actions, right mode of livelihood, right endeavour, right mindfulness, right concentration.[1]

We have already seen in our study of the Second Noble Truth the emphasis on deeds as creative for the future. The Fourth Noble Truth reinforces this with a programme of action, which, if followed, will lead to the cessation of pain with its frustrations, impermanence and lack of reality, in the attainment of Nirvana.

The word translated 'right' is the Pali word *samma*, of the same root as the Latin *summum*, meaning the highest or best. The eight factors in this Path fall under the three heads of wisdom or understanding, embracing right view and thought; ethical conduct expressed in right speech, action and livelihood; and mental discipline which includes right effort, mindfulness and concentration.

Right view consists in the right understanding of things as they are and particularly the Four Noble Truths covering the three characteristics of human life as full of ills, impermanent, and without abiding

[1] Translation by E. J. Thomas, *The Quest of Enlightenment.*

reality; the recognition of desire as the cause of man's pain; and the necessity to stop, reject and destroy desire in its many forms. Right view is more than just knowledge, it is penetration into the very nature of things.

Right thought is that from which all desire, hate and illusion have been eliminated, which is detached and selfless, patient and tolerant, calm and serene, free from all intentions of harming others, clear that when thought is right there will follow right speech and action.

The next group – right speech, action and livelihood – deals with conduct and is based on love and compassion. In one of his discourses the Buddha describes his own interpretation of right speech:

The recluse Gautama abstains from lying speech, he is a truth-speaker, a bondsman to truth, trustworthy, dependable, no deceiver of the world.

Abandoning slanderous speech, the recluse Gautama abstains from it; having heard something here, he is not one to repeat it elsewhere for causing variance. . . . In this way he is a reconciler of those who are at variance, one who combines those who are friends. Concord is his pleasure, his delight, his joy, concord is the motive of his speech.

Abandoning harsh speech, the recluse Gautama abstains from it. Whatever speech is gentle, pleasing to the ear, affectionate, going to the heart, urbane, pleasant and agreeable to the many-folk – such speech does he utter.

Abandoning frivolous chatter, the recluse Gautama abstains from it; he is a speaker at a right time, a speaker of fact, a speaker on the good, a speaker on *dhamma*, a speaker on discipline; he speaks words that are worth treasuring, with similes at the right times, words that are discriminating, connected with the goal.[1]

[1] *Dīgha-Nikāya* (PTS), i, 4–5.

Magga: The Way

Right action would include being friendly and compassionate to all living creatures, taking no life, of insect, animal or man; 'laying aside the cudgel and the sword', taking only what is given and waiting for it to be given, abstaining from all sexual impurity, promoting moral, honest and peaceful conduct, abstaining from intoxicating liquor which inflames the passions and dulls the mind and makes the body slothful.

Right livelihood means making one's living in ways that bring no harm to others. Any profession that involves killing should be abstained from such as that of soldier, butcher, fisherman, trading in arms or poisons, selling intoxicating drink.

This group of factors dealing with conduct is often summarized in the Five Great Commands binding on all Buddhists:

> To refrain from injury to living things.
> To refrain from taking that which is not given.
> To refrain from sexual immorality.
> To refrain from falsehood.
> To refrain from intoxicating liquors.

It may be commented that these commands are negative, but this is the beginning of moral discipline, as obvious in the Ten Commandments as in the Five Commands. The quotation and summaries above show that the Buddha interpreted them in a positive and searching way, to which students need to return if they are to be saved from the deadness of mere analysis.

The Buddhist ideal of the moral life is truly a noble one, yet the Buddhist finds it no easier to live up to it

G

than other people. In spite of the first precept which proclaims the sanctity of all life, human, animal or insect, the murder figures for Burma are among the highest in the world, and those in Ceylon are much the same. It seems as if the perversity of human nature, called to regard all life as sacred, succeeds only in reducing the value of human life to that of the animals. Dacoity is almost a seasonal problem, for the heat of the hot weather combined with the idleness that follows the harvesting of the rice crop, makes the hot season a time of anxiety for headmen and police, as well as a time of sad reflection for all who value the Noble Eightfold Path as the ideal. Christians, too, know how easy it is to fall short of the standards of right living of the Ten Commandments or of the more positive glory of God for each man's life. In the West we are conscious of a marked fall in moral standards – in truthfulness and honesty, in the disciplined control of sex, in faithfulness to marriage promises, and in the growing use of violence. Our prisons are full to overflowing and the level of delinquency among young people is disturbingly high. Christians would diagnose the cause of this in the drift away from religion; it looks as if moral stamina rises and falls with belief or lack of belief in a living God. Yet they would speak, humbly and gratefully, of a power that comes from God on which they can draw, grace sufficient for every temptation, failure, disaster or opportunity.

The third group of factors in the Fourth Noble Truth institutes the mental discipline, constantly emphasized

Magga: The Way

by the Buddha. Right Effort demands the energetic exercise of will to get rid of unwholesome and evil states of mind, to prevent them arising, and to produce and develop good and wholesome states of mind. 'Make what is right become' is a phrase that is repeated in the scriptures, often linked with its converse 'abandon what is wrong'. The Christian would regret with St Paul the weakness of will in most men, as in himself:

To will is present with me, but to do that which is good is not. For the good which I would I do not: but the evil which I would not, that I do.[1]

He would listen humbly to the Buddha's call to new efforts of will, he would admit that he has probably never exhausted the possibilities of human will within himself, he would also witness to the strengthening of the will within him when he has abandoned the lower self and opened the true self to the Spirit of God. Here he would see the relevance of Confirmation, the strengthening of the inner man, with the gifts of wisdom and understanding, counsel and spiritual strength, knowledge, true godliness and holy fear, so that he may achieve the purpose for which he was created and live the good life. The eightfold path sets out the programme of human action, the sevenfold gift brings the reinforcement of divine aid to the human will.

The second of the three constituents of mental discipline is right mindfulness, attentiveness or awareness, in which a whole course of training is involved. The

[1] Rom. 7.18–19.

training starts with concentrated attention on what
actually happens to us and in us, and embraces the
singling out for full attention of one after another of
the activities of the body, such as breathing or walking,
detailed examination of each feeling that arises within
us, and then a similar attention to each idea or thought
within the mind. This method of bare attention is
worked out at length in *The Heart of Buddhist Meditation* by Nyanaponika Thera; it is based on a discourse of
the Buddha entitled 'The Setting-up of Mindfulness'.
The learner is advised to begin by concentrating his
attention on some simple activity of the body, perhaps
the contracting of the muscles of the brow. He then
becomes aware of the relaxation of those muscles after
the tensing of them and the need of further relaxation.
The attention given must be as objective as possible,
without any subjective involvement, and as gentle as
possible, until gradually an alert passivity is attained in
which there is no effort or strain, but an acceptance of
what is happening and a surrender to it. This method
of concentrating on one bare point of attention may be
applied to awareness through any of the five senses. Its
result should be not only a growing skill in giving full,
unstrained attention, but a growing detachment from
ourselves, a new sense of receptivity and a relaxation and
peace for the body. The student may then proceed to a
similar practice of bare attention to a feeling – tension,
fear, irritation, joy, not trying to manipulate it in any
way, but becoming quietly aware of it, letting it make
its own impression. Similarly a thought in the mind

may be pin-pointed. This discipline gives a freedom from selfish preoccupation and brings about a right relationship to people and things. The author of Psalm 43 was practising it in some degree when he mused on the question, 'Why art thou so heavy, O my soul, and why art thou so disquieted within me?' Looking quietly at his mood of depression, detaching himself from it, he saw that in his case it was a subtle lack of trust, 'Put thy trust in God, for I shall yet praise him who is the help of my countenance and my God.'

The third factor in this group of Mental Discipline leads on naturally from Right Mindfulness to Right Concentration. There are four stages in it: in the first all desires, worries, lustful thoughts, ill-will and doubt are abandoned, and only feelings of good-will, peace and happiness allowed to remain; in the second, all cerebral activity is stilled, one-pointedness of mind is developed, all discursive thinking ceases and there is a happy sense of ease and joy; in the third stage the joy and happiness are no longer claimed, only the desire to become completely detached and receptive; finally comes the last stage, pure awareness of whatever reality there is, the timeless moment when time seems to stand still, the peace which passes all understanding.

Edward Conze in his *Buddhist Meditation*, while explaining and commending the Buddha's method of meditation does not feel hopeful of its practice in the modern world, where he sees a deep-rooted dislike for mental discipline, a pressure of time which means that only the professionals of the monastic life can follow

101

anything but the most elementary exercises, a level of noise which pursues men even into the quiet of the countryside, and the need of spiritual guides who will train and advise those ready to learn. Yet it is just this discipline and the peace that flows from it that people need not only for spiritual life but for mental health. A Harley Street doctor is using it in a way adapted for Western people and his psychiatric patients are gaining considerable benefit. Two schools of meditation have been opened in Rangoon where a steady stream of lay people put themselves under a monk, a meditation master for a whole month and learn what the novice learns in a good monastery. The experience of a visitor from the West in one of these schools of meditation is described in Admiral Shattock's *Experiment in Mindfulness*.

Zen Buddhism is attracting a considerable following in the West. The word Zen is the Japanese form of the Pali *Jhāna* and means meditation. In Zen meditation the aim is to stop all discursive thinking, to become open and receptive, so that there may come 'a moment of truth', a flash of illumination, a direct intuitive touch with reality. Obviously there are dangers of self-deception, and a wise and experienced teacher is needed.

What happens in the final moment of Meditation or *Jhāna*? the strict agnostic Buddhist, who believes neither in God nor an immortal soul, claims that he undergoes this experience of 'pure awareness' of the ultimate reality. The meditation technique of the Buddha can well be followed by Christians, who would say that in that final timeless moment they experience God, the self made in the image of God is brought into communion with its creator, that in those flashes of intuition, those moments of truth, God may speak.

In the higher stages of the Eightfold Path there is clearly a challenge to Christians to a discipline of meditation that few of us ever begin. There is also the need for the study and practice of it by a religious community, which, secure in its own experience of communion with God, is willing to try and enter into the experience of devout Buddhists. The practical approach might penetrate to the heart of the matter. Here is the Buddha's Way; some Christians must walk in it to find out where it leads.

10

The Sangha: The Third Gem

>>> ✧ <<<

THE word *Sangha* means 'community', but in general use it denotes the community or order of Buddhist monks. The Buddhist as he kneels before an image of the Buddha in the pagoda or monastery, or prepares himself for meditation in his own house or in some quiet spot, will begin by reverencing the Three Gems — the Buddha, the Dhamma and the Sangha. He will then in most cases go on to recite the Five Precepts or Great Commands. In the main countries of the Theravada tradition signs of the Buddhist religion meet the eye at almost every glance: the graceful tapering pagoda crowning any hill of eminence, in great centres like Rangoon covered with gold leaf shining in the sun by day and illuminated by night; the seven-tiered spire of the many monasteries, but above all the yellow robes of the monks as they make their morning round to beg their food from the homes of the faithful or as they move quietly and intently on some errand. In Burma out of a population of about 20 million people it is estimated that there are something like 60,000 monks, so the sight of the yellow robe is much more frequent than that of the clerical collar in a country like Britain.

How is it that the monks have come to be so honoured

and valued by the Buddhist laity, that in popular thinking good deeds done to them, such as the offering of daily food on the begging rounds or the provision of robes or the building of a monastery are looked upon as the most meritorious?

In the first place, the sight of the monk and his obvious withdrawal from the worldly affairs which occupy the attention of most people, is a reminder of the discipline of the senses and detachment from the world which is necessary in the lay life as well if any progress is to be made on the way that leads to the perfection of being and peace of Nirvana. The monk may only possess eight things – the three garments that make up his robe, a girdle, a begging bowl, a water-strainer to avoid swallowing living creatures, a razor to shave his head and a needle to repair his robes. He may not handle money.

O monk, empty this boat! if emptied, it will go quickly;
having cut off passion and hatred thou wilt go to Nirvana.[1]

The monk spends most of his time in study of the scriptures and in meditation, in his early years under the instruction of an experienced senior. In the morning he will go out, perhaps alone, more often as one of a file of monks, with his begging bowl, with downcast eyes, intent on his own thoughts, never uttering a word of thanks, for he is affording the lay supporters an opportunity of doing deeds which will produce good fruit in future lives. On his return to the monastery he will eat

[1] *Dhamma-pada*, 369.

105

his main meal of the day, from the food given in his begging bowl, or perhaps a more palatable meal, cooked by one of the attendant boys or a generous lay supporter, in which case the contents of the bowl will be fed to the boys or to the village dogs. The monk does no manual work, but he may teach in the school that always used to be attached to the monastery but is less so in these days of state education. He may also read the scriptures to lay people, teach them right mindfulness and meditation, and give them advice on the problems of life or on the practice of virtue. There are no set services for him to take or congregational worship as in a Christian church. At the new moon or the full moon there will be many more visitors to the monastery or pagoda and so better opportunities for explanation of the Dhamma. There will also be the great festivals, either of events in the life of the Buddha or local to the particular pagoda, when everyone is on holiday and generous people provide open hospitality, either in their own homes or in temporary bamboo pavilions, for all who like to come, the monks being entertained at a specially raised dais.

There are two monastic practices which have survived from the time of the Buddha. The first is the *uposatha* or fortnightly chapter at which each monk confesses his infringements of the 227 rules of the *Vinaya*, the book of discipline of the monks, which is one of the three main sections of the *Pitakas* or scriptures. The second is the observance of the Buddhist Lent covering the three months of the Rainy Season, which must be spent in retreat. During this time all travelling is forbidden.

The Sangha: The Third Gem

The Sangha also plays an important part in the ceremony of admission to the Order, when a young lad is escorted in procession round the town or villages, dressed in princely robes to recall the Buddha's withdrawal from his father's court in search of the truth about pain. On arrival at the monastery the young man takes off his princely robes, and is clothed in the robes of the monk, his head is shaven and he places himself under obedience to the abbot. As almost every boy in the Theravada countries becomes a monk for some period in his life, the influence of the Sangha can be well understood. Monks, too, will be present at funerals, and one or more of them will read passages from the scriptures or preach a sermon dealing with the impermanence of human life.

Above all the monk aims at detachment and serenity within himself:

Putting away the hankering after the world, he remains with a heart that hankers not, and purifies his mind of lusts. Putting away the corruption of the wish to injure, he remains with a heart free from ill-temper, and purifies his mind of malevolence. Putting away torpor of heart and mind, keeping his ideas alight, mindful and self-possessed, he purifies his mind of weakness and of sloth. Putting away flurry and worry, he remains free from fretfulness, and with heart serene within, he purifies himself of irritability and vexation of spirit. Putting away wavering, he remains as one passed beyond perplexity; and no longer in suspense as to what is good, he purifies his mind of doubt.[1]

[1] *Dialogues of the Buddha* (Sacred Books of the Buddhists), OUP p. 82.

'With his heart thus serene, he directs and bends down his mind to the knowledge which penetrates the heart. Penetrating with his own heart the hearts of other beings, of other men, he knows them, he discerns whether they are passionate or calm, angry or peaceful, dull or alert, mind attentive or wandering, mean or lofty, steadfast or wavering, free or enslaved.'[1] The Christian would recognize here the gentle but incisive touch of a father confessor, who has progressed in the spiritual life and can from his own experience help those on the earlier stages of the path.

In one of the Buddha's sermons the good monk is likened to a skilful oarsman with a sturdy boat, equipped with sound oars and rudder, who launches his boat on the stormy sea towards the farther shore. Other men seeing him will learn the kind of boat they need and how to row it.

Helpers on the Way, the Noble Eightfold Path, would be another fitting description of the good monk, always recognizing that there will be some concentrating on their own progress and others whose hearts do not measure up to the ideals of the yellow robe which they wear.

Perhaps the reverence given to the monks by the laity is seen most clearly at the funeral of a monk, which is one of the most joyful occasions in the religious life of Buddhists in Burma. The body will have been embalmed and kept until an appropriate day, when it will be placed on a wonderful erection of bamboo, decorated with tinsel and paper, ready for cremation. The lighting of

[1] Ibid., p. 92.

the funeral pyre is the signal for fireworks and great jubilation for everyone is quite certain that the holy monk has now finished the cycle of existence and will return to earth no more but will enter into the great peace of Nirvana. The watching monks who know their own hearts and perhaps their dead colleague may possibly doubt this, but there is no doubt about their hope and longing.

In Theravada countries like Burma, it is generally assumed that to reach the goal of Nirvana at the end of the Eightfold Path it is necessary to become a monk. Thus it is not uncommon for an elderly Burman, who has raised a family and provided for them, and completed his public service, to forsake the world, take the monk's robe and spend his declining years in the discipline of the monastery which will advance him on the road to Arahantship (saint-hood) and Nirvana. Yet modern Buddhist writers are emphasizing teaching of the Buddha which seems to imply the possibility of laymen achieving this goal.

One day the Blessed One was asked by a layman:

'Must I give up my wealth, my home and my business enterprises and, like you, go into homelessness in order to attain the bliss of the religious life?'

The Buddha replied:

'The bliss of the religious life is attainable by everyone who walks in the noble eightfold path. He that cleaves to wealth had better cast it away than allow his heart to be poisoned by it; but he who does not cleave to wealth, and possessing riches uses them rightly, will be a blessing unto his fellow-beings.

'I say unto thee, remain in thy station of life and apply thyself with diligence to thy enterprises. It is not life and wealth and power that enslave men, but the cleaving to life and wealth and power.

'The Dhamma of the Tathagata does not require a man to go into homelessness or to resign the world unless he feels called upon to do so; but the Dhamma of the Tathāgata requires every man to free himself from the illusion of self, to cleanse his heart, to give up his thirst for pleasure, and lead a life of righteousness.'[1]

On another occasion, the Buddha assured his monks that a particular householder had gone to fulfilment and had seen and realized the Deathless, because he was endowed with six necessary things: unwavering confidence in the Buddha himself, unwavering confidence in Dhamma and unwavering confidence in the Sangha, together with noble moral discipline, knowledge and freedom.

There is in the scriptures and increasingly being mentioned in modern writings a wider interpretation of the Sangha, as the community of those who travel along the Eightfold Path and have some touch with the holy ones who have attained enlightenment, and whom they earnestly desire to join.

The early Buddhists believed in a number of other worlds. First of all there is a world of nature gods, the governors of the four quarters of the firmament and the

---

[1] Quoted by G. Appleton, *Buddhism in Burma*, Longmans, Burma Pamphlets, 1943.

personification of sun, moon, etc. Then there is the world of the thirty councillors with Sakka as their Governor, probably to be identified with Indra. Thirdly there is the world of Yamas or Watchers, where men passing from the earth through death hear their fate. Here they are reminded of the three messengers – a sick person, an old person and a dead body, sights which had so much effect on the young Gautama, and which should have warned those now standing before Yama's judgement seat of the need to avoid evil and seek good. In other mentions in the scriptures two other signs are added, that of a monk as presumably the right way of life and that of a new-born man as the alternative of a further life in the world. Yama's judgement may result in a return to this world or a period in the Tusita heavens of the happy righteous beings or a period in hell, the tortures of which the scriptures describe in lurid details. These tortures are pictured in many pagodas in Burma as a warning to evildoers, but the most significant point about the Buddhist hell is that it is only temporary. There are four other worlds of gods or devas, who are not gods in any theistic sense, but only beings like ourselves, yet with some power of making themselves known to beings in other worlds including our own and of being some help to them. After a spell in one of these worlds men return to this for a further round of opportunity. In Christian terms the Buddhist gods are more like angels, the heavens correspond to paradises, and the hells are more like purgatory than any sphere of eternal damnation.

There is a good deal of coming and going between this world and the others, and some lovely touches in the scriptures speak of the welcome given to worthy men on their arrival from this world at one of the happy heavens: 'Come, Sir! Welcome, Sir! Long is it since you made occasion to come this way. Be seated! here is a seat ready!'

Mrs Rhys Davids says of these other worlds:

If once we see in the devas of the early Sakyan days the fellow-men at a different stage in life's becoming from 'the man' just now on earth, it may dawn upon us that here we have a notable anticipation of the Christian ideal worded as 'the Communion of Saints' – a confraternity of the very worthy, linking world with world, and holding up, it may be, a light in our darkness. Too much, may be, do we relegate that saintly communion to a vague hereafter; too little is the forward Way, for us, a wayfaring *with* the kindly warding devas of a better world.[1]

The Bible speaks of bright messengers from another world, bringing messages and insights to men and women receptive to God, bringing help to men in times of difficulty and need; it also speaks of the spirits of just men made perfect and concerned that we should play our part as courageously as they did:

Therefore, let us also, seeing we are compassed about with so great a cloud of witnesses, lay aside every weight, and the sin which doth so easily beset us, and let us run with patience the race that is set before us, looking unto Jesus, the author and perfecter of our faith, who for the joy that was set before him endured the cross, despising the shame, and hath sat down at the right hand of the throne of God.[2]

[1] Mrs Rhys Davids, *Sakya*, p. 285. [2] Heb. 12.1–2.

The Sangha: The Third Gem

The Christian believes that he sees more clearly than the Buddhist what is at the end of the road – and it is a Person, one who came forth from eternity, lived life in this world in the light of eternity, accepted the deepest depths of suffering, returned to eternity, blazing a way for men to follow, to the very heart of eternity which is the Presence of God. Christ as the Way begins at the beginning of things and he goes beyond the Eightfold Path, to the end of all things. In between, the two Paths have much in common.

11

Life in the World

>>> ✧ <<<

I⊤ is often said by people in the West that Buddhism is
a religion of world-negation; equally often it is assumed
by Buddhists in the East that the life of the monk is the
only one that will lead to Nirvana and that therefore
people must withdraw from the world. This was certainly
not so in the days of the Buddha, for the Scriptures show
him as frequently concerned with rulers and merchants,
bankers and householders, farmers and cowherds, men
women and young people involved in the affairs of daily
life.

In one of the discourses of the Buddha there is a lovely
description of the good life; it is called the Song of
Blessing and is known and loved by every Burmese
Buddhist:

One night a spirit came to the Blessed one and addressed him
thus in verse:
Many devas and men have pondered on blessings,
Longing for goodly things. O tell me Thou the greatest
blessing.

The Lord replied:

Not to follow after fools, but to follow after the wise;
The worship of the worshipful, – this is the greatest blessing.

Life in the World

To dwell in a pleasant spot, to have done good deeds in former
  births,
To have set oneself in the right path, – this is the greatest
  blessing.

Much learning and much science, and a discipline well learned,
Yea, and a pleasant utterance, – this is the greatest blessing.

The support of mother and father, the cherishing of child and
  wife,
To follow a peaceful livelihood, – this is the greatest blessing.

Giving alms, the righteous life, to cherish kith and kin,
And to do deeds that bring no blame, – this is the greatest
  blessing.

Reverence, humility, content, and gratitude,
To hear the Law at proper times, – this is the greatest blessing.

Patience, the soft answer, the sight of those controlled,
And pious talk in season due, – this is the greatest blessing.

Restraint, the holy life, discernment of the Noble Truths,
Of one's own self to know the Goal, – this is the greatest
  blessing.

A heart untouched by worldly things, a heart that is not
  swayed
By sorrow, a heart passionless, secure, – this is the greatest
  blessing.

Invincible on every side, they go who do these things,
On every side they go to bliss, – theirs is the greatest blessing.[1]

[1] Translated by F. L. Woodward, *Some Sayings of the Buddha*,
OUP, World Classics, 1925.

'The cherishing of child and wife – reverence, humility content and gratitude . . . patience, the soft answer – the holy life – a heart untouched by worldly things, a heart that is not swayed by sorrow.' The Christian wayfarer through life rejoices as he sees these lovely things on the Buddhist Path; they are familiar to him through St Paul's list of the fruits of the Spirit: 'love, joy, peace, patience, kindness, goodness, faithfulness, gentleness, self control'.[1] When these are in the heart no external law is needed. To the Buddhist such inner virtues will result in a harvest of good deeds: to the Christian they are the harvest of the Holy Spirit within the spirit or true self. St Paul says that these virtues only come when the flesh or lower nature with its passions and desires has been crucified. The Buddhist strives for them, so does the Christian; the latter speaks of his experience that there is a power from without that helps these things to grow. He goes even further and believes that the seed of them is implanted within man's being by that power, to which the Buddhist asserts once more the need of man's will and effort.

The Buddha's evaluation of the layman's life, with its family and social implications is seen in another sermon attributed to him. One day he came across a young man, Sigāla, who had not found any real satisfaction in the religious life he saw around him, but in obedience to the wishes of his father expressed on his deathbed, was paying honour to the six cardinal points of the heavens. The Buddha spoke to him of the noble

[1] Gal. 5.22.

116

discipline of his own teaching in which the six directions worthy of worship were 'parents as the east, teachers as the south, wife and children as the west, friends and companions as the north, servants and work people as the nadir, religious teachers and brahmans as the zenith'.

In each of these relationships five duties are enumerated:

The child's duty to his parents:

Once supported by them I will now be their support; I will perform duties incumbent on them; I will keep up the lineage and tradition of my family; I will make myself worthy of my heritage.

The parents' love for him is explained:

They restrain him from vice, they exhort him to virtue, they train him to a profession, they contract a suitable marriage for him, and in due time they hand over his inheritance.

Pupils minister to their teachers:

By rising (from their seat, in salutation) by waiting upon them, by eagerness to learn, by personal service, and by attention when receiving their teaching.

Teachers reciprocate in love:

They train him in that wherein he has been well trained; they make him hold fast that which is well held; they thoroughly instruct him in the lore of every art; they speak well of him among his friends and companions. They provide for his safety in every quarter.

A husband ministers to his wife 'by respect, by courtesy, by faithfulness, by handing over authority to her, by providing her with adornment.' The wife in return carries out her duties well, provides hospitality to the kin of both, is faithful, watches over the goods he brings home, and discharges her business with skill and industry.

A man carries out his duty to his friends 'by generosity, courtesy and benevolence, by treating them as he treats himself, and by being as good as his word', while his friends respond by protecting him when he is off his guard, by guarding his property on such occasions, by being a refuge for him in danger, by not forsaking him in his troubles, and by showing consideration for his family.

A good master gives his servants work according to their strength, supplies them with food and wages, tends them in sickness, shares with them unusual delicacies, and grants them spare time each day and occasional leave. Servants for their part rise early, go to bed late, are content with what is given them, do their work well, and care for their master's good fame.

The duty towards religious teachers is observed 'by affection in act and speech and mind, by keeping open house to them, by supplying their temporal needs'. In return, recluses and brahmans show their love to the layman in six ways: 'they restrain him from evil, they exhort him to good, they love him with kindly thoughts; they teach him what he had not heard, they correct and purify what he has heard, they reveal to him the way to heaven'.[1]

[1] Summarized from *Dialogues of the Buddha*, Part III (Sacred Books of the Buddhists), OUP, pp. 180–83.

Life in the World

It has been thought right to summarize this teaching at some length for it presupposes an approval of the life of layfolk in the world and furnishes a very good pattern of attitude and behaviour. T. W. Rhys Davids comments, 'Happy would have been the village or clan on the banks of the Ganges, where the people were full of the fellow-feeling, the noble spirit of justice which breaches through these naïve and simple sayings,' to which his wife adds, 'Not less happy would be the village, or the family on the banks of the Thames today, of which this could be said.'

For a man who spent fifty years as a monk as the Buddha did these quotations show a keen knowledge of the life of ordinary people and a delightfully human way of speaking about it, which make his teaching as relevant and compelling today as it was 2,500 years ago. One more lovely human passage must be allowed, some teaching for girls approaching marriageable age, which the Christian will put alongside the praise of the virtuous woman in the Book of Proverbs, whose price is above rubies:

Therefore, girls, train yourselves thus: To whatever husband our parents shall give us — anxious for our good, seeking our happiness, compassionate, out of compassion — for him we will rise up early, be the last to retire, be willing workers, order all things sweetly and speak affectionately. Train yourselves thus, girls.

And in this way also, girls: We will be deft and nimble at our husband's home-crafts, whether they be of wool or cotton, making it our business to understand the work, so as to do it and get it done. Train yourselves thus, girls.

And in this way also, girls: Whatever our husband's household consists of – servants or messengers or workpeople – we will know the work of each one of them by what has been done and their remissness by what has not been done; . . . Train yourselves thus, girls.

And in this way also, girls: The treasure, corn, silver, and gold that our husband brings home, we will keep safe watch and ward over it, and will act as no robber, thief, carouser or wastrel in regard to it. Train yourselves thus, girls.[1]

The rewards of this on the breaking-up of the body after dying, will be rebirth among the *devas* of lovely form! Clearly, mother and wife had taught Gautama something about woman's nature before he made the great renunciation. Yet perhaps it must be added that the promise is only a happy period in one of the heavens; Nirvana lies more than one lifetime ahead.

The Buddha was not content to deal only with personal, family and social life, he was interested also in good government. In a discourse entitled 'The Ten Duties of the King' he sets out rules which should be of great interest to statesmen, politicians, members of parliament and government officials, especially in newly-independent countries of Buddhist background like Burma and Ceylon.

The Ten Duties are well summarized by Rahula,[2] whose book shows a striking application of Buddhist principles to modern conditions:

[1] *Anguttara-Nikāya* (PTS), iii, 37-8 as quoted in *The Living Thoughts of Gotama the Buddha* by A. K. Coomaraswamy and I. B. Horner.

[2] Op. cit., pp. 84–85.

Life in the World

1. Generosity and charity. The ruler should have no attachment to property or wealth, but give it away for the benefit of the people.
2. High moral character. He should observe the Five Precepts: never destroy life, cheat, steal and exploit others, commit adultery, lie or take intoxicating drinks.
3. He should sacrifice comfort, fame, and life itself, if necessary, for the welfare of the people.
4. Honesty and integrity, free from fear or favour, not deceiving the public.
5. He should be kind and gentle.
6. He should lead a life of self-control and austerity, not indulging in luxury.
7. Freedom from all hatred and ill-will, bearing no grudge against anyone.
8. Non-violence, harming nobody, trying to avoid violence, war, destruction of life.
9. Patience and understanding. He should bear hardships, difficulties and insults without losing his temper.
10. He should not oppose the will of the people but do everything conducive to their welfare.

One great king, Asoka, who ruled over the Maurya empire in India in the third century B.C. tried to put these principles into practice. After his victorious war against the Kalingas in 261 B.C., in which many thousands of men lost their lives, the horrors of war so impressed him that he decided to devote himself to the spread of Buddhism, first as a lay adherent and later as a monk. We can learn much of the Buddhist principles on which he tried to rule, from edicts which he caused to be inscribed on rocks and pillars, many of which still exist today. He abolished sacrificial slaughter, advocated the humane treatment of criminals and animals, caused wells to be dug and rest-houses to be built, and arranged for the care and healing of the sick. He also sent Buddhist missionaries to North-West India, Nepal and Ceylon and possibly further afield. The Edicts bear witness to Asoka's ideals for the officials of his Kingdom who 'have been created for the welfare and happiness of the country, with intent that fearlessly, confidently and quietly they may perform their duties'. It is interesting to note that capital punishment was retained, for there is provision in one edict for a respite of three days to condemned men lying in prison under sentence of death, so that they may be invited to deep meditation and other religious duties 'with a view to the other world'.

Thus there is in the teaching of the Buddha and in early Buddhist history plenty of material to show that in the early generations Buddhism was not regarded as a way of escape from life in the world, nor as a selfish way of gaining a better status in the next life. The independence achieved by Buddhist countries in recent years is focussing attention once more on the application of the Buddha's teaching to social and national duties, and its emphasis on 'non-harming', backed up by the example of Asoka, who in his hour of victory and strength renounced war and territorial conquest, challenges the nations of the West to a similar agreement. Part of the strength of Buddhism today lies in its charge of failure on the part of Christianity to lead the so-called Christian nations into the way of peace. Buddhist nations have gone to war in the past as the history of Burma and Siam will show, and in modern times Japan, with a strong Buddhist element in its national character, has been guilty of aggression. Buddhist statesmen in posts of leadership will realize the responsibility of the use of power, both for internal and external security. Buddhism, as emphatically as Christianity, will recognize the things that belong unto peace – justice, righteousness, truth, right intention and peaceful means of change, so that swords may be beaten into ploughshares, spears into pruning hooks, tanks into tractors, and nuclear generators used for irrigating the desert and providing light and power.

The Union of Burma has a plan for making Buddhism the State religion: U Nu its Prime Minister, a devout Buddhist, often expresses the wish to retire from the pressure and problems of political life into the peace of the monastery, but in a truly Buddhist spirit he stays on in public life at the request of his countrymen and for the sake of his country. He has worked for internal unity and for peaceful relations with other nations. He is tolerant and understanding in his attitude to other religions, and is eager that Burma should not become a purely secular and materialistic nation. He believes that if its national life is based on the principles of the Buddha, Burma will be a righteous and united country, able to make a contribution of its own to the community of nations. Others who are loudly demanding that Buddhism shall become the State religion are not as truly Buddhist in their outlook, but are motivated more by narrowly nationalist sentiments, so that some

Christians have feared that there is a danger of people of other religions being ranked as second-class citizens. If Buddhist principles prevail, as U Nu wants them to do, Christians and others need not fear that their rights under the constitution will be affected, nor that they will not be given their due share in public posts.

If Buddhism becomes the State religion, there will undoubtedly be some state patronage of monasteries, support for the training of monks, the encouragement of the highest standards of learning and discipline in the Sangha, education and training in the Buddhist religion in State schools, and an emphasis on the working out of the Five Great Commands in personal and national life. A truly Buddhist state would be a most interesting experiment, and the statesman who brought it into being would go down to history as a modern Asoka. Christians, in the period of decision, would voice a note of caution, not in any narrow, defensive spirit, but anxious lest religion should come too much under the control of the State and so lose its freedom of spirit and action. If the Buddhist State finally comes into being, Christians will continue to bring their insights of the Kingdom of God to the building-up of the national life.

Buddhists expect a fifth and final Buddha, to see whose coming is regarded by the devout as the greatest blessing. The desire of Buddhists in Tibet and Mongolia for the coming of Maitreya is seen in the countless inscriptions on mountain rocks, 'Come, Maitreya, come', a desire movingly close to the prayer of Christians in the apostolic age, and indeed in later ages, 'Come, Lord

Life in the World

Jesus, come'. A Burmese monk described the coming of Maitreya in these words:

As the last Buddha was the Lord of Wisdom, so the next Buddha will be the Lord of Love. The mountains will be levelled, and the world become a vast plain full of orchards, gardens and rice-fields. Man then will be without any enemy among men, and without fear of ravening beasts. It will be the age of plenty and good-will.

Strangely reminiscent of the golden age of the book of Isaiah and of the intuition which came from another world to some shepherds on the Bethlehem hillside

Peace on earth, to men of good will.

12

The Beyond

>>> ✧ <<<

THE Christian wayfarer on the Noble Eightfold Path will have seen many admirable things, he will have reverenced the figure of the Buddha with his love of men, with his diagnosis of what is wrong with man, with his distrust of religious beliefs and practices, with his emphasis on man's responsibility for his own salvation, and his insistence on limiting attention to what falls within man's experience. He will have been thrilled with parallels between the Buddha and the Christ, and recognized that the ethical standards enjoined by each come very close to one another. Yet he will also have noticed certain differences, two of which constantly recur — the question of the self and the existence of God.

If the strict Thera-vadin view is accepted that there is no self, except that which is nothing more than an ever-changing stream of thoughts, feelings, consciousness and desire, then there is little more to be said. All that is left is to pit two contradictory opinions against each other. We agree to differ completely and radically. If there is no true self in man, it is a waste of time to search for the source of true self-hood. If there is no permanent self then the only destiny for man is to sink back into some undifferentiated common ground. Indeed, Dr Kraemer suggests that the logical development of the Hindu belief in the identity of the spirit in man with the impersonal divine spirit is the atheism of Thera-vada Buddhism and its rejection of an eternal self.

But as we have seen, this is not the only possible Buddhist view, however strongly it may be held by Singalese and German Buddhists today. The scriptures speak of a false idea of self; they also speak of a self that is dear, that is to be a man's refuge and guide, that is to be lord of the other self. We have seen too that this deeper self can be experienced, and that when it takes over the government of the empirical, conscious self, the result is integration and liberation or new birth. On this view it is reasonable to explore the source of true self-hood.

It is here that the experience of Moses is relevant. One day while shepherding his flocks on the slopes of Mount Sinai he sees a burning bush. The bush is not consumed, so it is no ordinary bush of nature. It is transfigured, ablaze with glory, and 'as he stands before it Moses feels that there is a presence there. So compelling is this feeling that he takes off his sandals, the act of reverence of a Muslim before he enters the mosque or a Buddhist before he goes into a pagoda or monastery. As he stands there rapt with awe and wonder, an intuition arises within him that he is to return to Egypt to rescue his people. The experience, however, is more than subjective; there is the sense of someone other, speaking to him with authority, someone with whom he may

speak. So he voices a first difficulty: 'You are sending
me to the children of Israel; they will want to know my
credentials. When they ask me what is the name of the
God who has sent me, what shall I say to them?' The
reply comes: 'You shall say I AM has sent me to you.'[1]
That is all that is to be said, all that can be said, all that
needs to be said – I AM.

To the Jew, the Christian and the Muslim God is the
one eternal, self-existent Being, the only one who can
say 'I am' in his own right. He is the ground of all
existence, the source of all self-hood. The poem of
creation in the first chapter of Genesis says that man is
made in the image of God – in his true being he is akin
to God. There is something in him, it may be only in
seed-form, that enables him to recognize God and to
respond when God speaks. In many cases men run away
from God or hide from him. In the story of man's fall,
so psychologically true, Adam after his first disobedience
hides himself from God, and God comes to seek him,
calling, 'Adam, where art thou?'

In another story, this time in the New Testament,
man has to come to himself before he can come to God –
'But when he came to himself he said . . . I will arise
and go to my father.'[2] The parable of the Prodigal Son,
while being perhaps the most Christian of all stories, has
a Buddhist note about it: the son reaps the harvest of his
deeds; he sees the worthlessness and purposelessness of
the life to which he has arrived; he resolves to return
home, and it must have taken great exertion of will

[1] See Ex. 3.13–14.   [2] Luke 15.17, 18.

especially the last mile. As he nears his home he sees his father running towards him with outstretched arms. There a Christian may see a connection between the Buddha and the Christ. A man must become disillusioned with the false self, the ego; he must find the true self deep down within his being. Then he may find God.

The process of salvation in Christian terms, of liberation in Buddhist terms, of integration in psychological terms, must begin within man, in the exertion of his will. Then he finds someone coming to meet him, to show him the way, to bring reinforcement to the will, the assurance that the universe is on his side. At first the movement of the will may be only a feeble flicker – without it nothing can happen. However weak, it is the signal for an in-rush of power. A helpless paralytic had to be carried to Jesus by his four friends[1] – paralysed and palsied he lay on his pallet, brought there by the sins of the past. Jesus assures him that men need not be the prisoners of the past, because God comes to restore a broken relationship and to bring a 'more' into his life. Then comes the stern command of love – 'Arise, take up thy bed and go unto thy house!', demanding a response of will. The two things were necessary – the movement of the human will and the reinforcement from the divine will – not one, or the other, but both. Perhaps the onlookers could see this wreck of a man make the first effort to brace the long disused muscles – and at once new power came flooding in. He struggled to his feet, rolled up his pallet and walked back to his house.

[1] See Mark 2.3–12.

Told in these words the process of salvation might seem to be nothing more than a human response to God coming from without. But the New Testament is equally emphatic that the divine initiative also operates within man. The very movement of man's will is divinely initiated, for man in his inmost being is made in the image of God and the Spirit of God is constantly pressing in upon both conscious and subconscious. Once again we come back to the biblical faith in man as created in the image of God. One of the characteristics of this divine pattern is the possession of will – given by God in the first place at each man's birth, and moved by God to respond to God's coming from without. Often, men are ignorant of the will within themselves, often they mistake for it the egocentric self which has to be repudiated, often it has become so weak in its enslavement to the lower self that only a flicker is left. Yet God moves within that flicker, and when man responds, great things begin to happen. Christians speak of this action within the spirit of man as grace, the work of God himself within the spirit that he has created, which belongs to him, and which even in the deepest selfishness or degradation retains a trace of its divine ancestry. Yet man is always free and can always say 'no' to God. God has made him free and will not withdraw this most precious of all his gifts, but hopes for the willing and glad consent of his creatures. God always stands at the door and knocks; he never forces his way in, but waits for the tenant to open the door and invite him to come in.

Emphasis on the will of man is magnificently stressed

in Buddhism; the origin and the implications of will need to be equally stressed. Unless they are, man is in danger of falling into what the Christian regards as the sin of all sins, to make a god of himself, his original and perennial temptation. Conversion comes when a man surrenders his will to the will of God, 'Lord, what wilt thou have me to do?' is the moment when a man accepts salvation; 'Not my will, but thine be done' is the gladly accepted principle of the new life; and the unlimited infusing of God's grace is the consequence. Man then becomes, in Buddhist terms, a *jina*, more than conqueror, in every situation. From henceforth his *Dhamma* or guiding light is the Will of God.

The principle of a two-way traffic, interaction of the human and the divine, can be seen in another way in the relationship of Christianity and Buddhism. Both believe in an additional dimension of human life — living in the light of eternity. To the Buddhist this is symbolized by Nirvana towards which he travels by the noble eightfold path, trying to break into it, as it were, by sheer determination. To the Christian this dimension is found in God: to him God in Christ has broken into human existence bringing eternal life with him. The Buddha is said to have experienced Nirvana in this life and to have entered into Pari-nirvana, full and perfect bliss, at his death. The Christian can experience eternal life now: to him it comes from knowing God, not just in second-hand knowledge about God, but in entering into personal experience of God. 'And this is eternal life, that they should know thee, the only true God, and him whom thou didst send, even Jesus Christ.'[1] Nirvana is, to the Buddhist, eternity: Jesus Christ, to the Christian, *is* eternity.

The Christian on the frontier is heartened to find a kindly Buddhist there in Dr Suzuki, the veteran Zen scholar of Japan. His book, *Mysticism: Christian and Buddhist*, makes a deep study of Christian mystics like Eckhart, Vaughan and Traherne and compares their writings with those of Zen mystics. He is concerned to find the spiritual reality behind the symbols, both Christian and Buddhist, and his thought brings light and confirmation to Christian as well as to Buddhist, as when he says:

The Biblical God is said to have given his name to Moses on Mount Sinai as 'I am that I am'. This is a most profound utterance, for all our religious or spiritual or metaphysical experiences start from it. This is the same as Christ's saying, 'I am', that is, he is eternity itself, while Abraham is in time, therefore, he 'was' and not 'is'. Those who live in the light of eternity always are and are never subjected to the becoming of 'was' and 'will be'.[2]

Quoting Sermon 18 of Meister Eckhart, he helps Christian and Buddhist to understand the Christian conviction that the true self is Christ begotten by God in the human soul:

In eternity, the Father begets the Son in his own likeness. 'The Word was with God and the Word was God.' Like

[1] John 17.3.
[2] D. T. Suzuki, *Mysticism: Christian and Bhuddist*, Allen and Unwin, p. 112.

God, it had his nature. Furthermore, I say that God has
begotten him in my soul. Not only is the soul like him and
he like it, but he is in it, for the Father begets his Son in the
soul exactly as he does in eternity and not otherwise. He
must do so whether he will or not. The Father ceaselessly
begets his Son and, what is more, he begets me not only as
his Son but as himself and himself as myself, begetting me
in his own nature, his own being. At that inmost Source, I
spring from the Holy Spirit and there is one life, one being,
one action. All God's works are one and therefore he begets
me as he does his Son and without distinction.[1]

To this Dr Suzuki adds his own comment: 'We must
not forget that the truth of Eckhart's sermon comes
from setting ourselves in the light of eternity. As long
as we are creatures in time and seeking our own and
not God's will, we shall never find God in ourselves.'[2]

He even quotes Eckhart to support Christians in their
conviction of creatureliness, thus strengthening us for
the dialogue with Hindus in their belief in the identity
of God and the human soul or with some Buddhists who
hold that man's final destiny is to sink back into the
undifferentiated common ground.

The union of the soul with God is far more inward than that
of the soul and body. . . . Now, I might ask, how stands it
with the soul that is lost in God? Does the soul find herself
or not? To this I will answer as it appears to me, that the soul
finds herself in the point where every rational being under-
stands itself with itself. Although it sinks in the eternity of
the divine essence, yet it can never reach the ground.
Therefore God has left a little point wherein the soul turns

[1] Quoted from Blakney, *Translation of Eckhart's Works*, Harper
and Brothers, p. 181.   [2] Op. cit., p. 112

back upon itself and finds itself, and knows itself to be a creature.[1]

God provides us with a 'little point', so that we may realize that we are finite creatures who can never sink into 'the essence of God'. When we come to our true selves we know that we originate from God, that we are akin to God, that God through Christ lives in us. Each one of us can now say 'I am', and if we continue in that experience and in dependence upon the I AM we too shall be eternal, in union with God, yet still ourselves and still creatures.

Are there any further Buddhist reasons that make belief in God reasonable? In the discussions on Nirvana between King Milinda and the monk Nagasena, quoted in chapter 8, the King asks the monk whether he could prove . . .

the dimension of Nirvana by analogy, reason, logic or demonstration. The monk puts a counter question and asks the king whether he believes that there is a 'formless god' in the realm of the formless. 'Yes,' says the king, 'I have heard of such a god.' 'Well then,' continues the monk, 'can you prove the form, the existence, and the dimensions of that god by analogy, reason, logic or demonstration?' 'No Lord,' the king humbly submits, but affirms, that in spite of not being able to prove the existence of that god that this formless god does exist. 'Even so, O King,' concludes Nagasena the monk, 'the existence, form and dimensions of Nirvana, which exists in its own right, cannot be proved by analogy, reason, logic or demonstration. Nirvana cannot be verified

[1] Quoted from W. R. Inge, *Mysticism in Religion*, Hutchinson, 1947, p. 39.

The Beyond

in any literal sense, but it is a firm well grounded belief of all Buddhists. The supposed unverifiability of God is logically in the same position.'[1]

In one of the books of the *Abhi-dhamma Pitaka*, which deals with psychological ethics, four spheres of consciousness are analysed, of which the highest is the supramundane sphere, 'the sphere of infinite consciousness'. In this sphere alone there is a special constituent of consciousness, 'the insight that makes for the realization of those truths that are unrealized, uncomprehended, unknown'. It would seem therefore that there are values which cannot be known in the physical sphere, which can however be known in the spiritual sphere, where there is no limit to what can be known. May we not therefore infer that God can be known in this spiritual sphere where he reveals himself? May we not even claim that we have experienced God, and that therefore Buddhists who base so much on experience, should be prepared to examine an experience which is common to Christians, Jews and Muslims?

Theravada Buddhists will find evidence and experience from their brethren of the Mahayana School which may suggest the need to reconsider the question of the existence of an Eternal God. For in Mahayana Buddhism the Buddha who never claimed to be divine, has become a God, and a God in Trinity. This Trinity consists firstly of the Dhamma-body, the self-subsistent reality, what Buddhists call Buddhahood and what

[1] Summarized in CPCL Pamphlet No. 2, Lynn de Silva, *Belief in God*.

Christians call Godhead; secondly, the Body of Enjoyment, through which he reveals himself in successive Buddhas in different universes, an idea coming close to that of the Eternal Christ, the Word through whom God has revealed himself all through the ages; and thirdly, the Body of Transfiguration, the incarnate God as it were, the human Buddha who taught and lived the Four Noble Truths in the sixth century B.C.

Zaehner rightly comments on this:

The transformation of Buddhism from an original atheism into a constellation of theistic systems proves not that the empirical psychology of the human Buddha was untrue; it proves only that it was not fully satisfying to the psychological constitution of the average man, for it leaves out of account the psychological needs of the great majority of the human race; it ignores their need to worship.[1]

Some Buddhists in Tibet and Nepal have developed the idea of a supreme Buddha, omnipotent and omniscient, who is the First Cause of the Universe. To this primeval Buddha they gave the name of Adi-Buddha; he is also described as the 'Womb of the Tathāgatas', the ultimate reality from which both the Universe and the line of succeeding Buddhas are said to issue. Edward Conze says that this belief developed about 1000 A.D. when Buddhists in North-West India came into contact with the conquering forces of Islam, and desired to be all things to all men. In his judgement such a development can only result in a merging with monotheistic religions.

[1] Zaehner, *At Sundry Times*, Faber and Faber, 1958, p. 104.

The Beyond

These theistic developments do not prove the existence of God, they only suggest that the cold, impersonal, non-theistic system of Theravada Buddhism does not satisfy the spiritual needs of men. On a more simple and human level many Buddhists in Burma think of the Buddha much as Christians think of Jesus Christ, praying to him and looking for his merit and help in their efforts to tread the Eightfold Path.

The question of why Buddhism lost the place of influence which it once held in India also needs to be asked. Undoubtedly the entrenched position of the Brahmans and their hostility to what seemed a new and rival system was a main factor. But the development of belief that there was no divine *Ātman* or Eternal Spirit in the Universe, and no *ātman* or soul in man, was directly contrary to the central emphasis of Indian religious thought, which is the relationship of the Spirit of God to the spirit of man. This Personalist Controversy, as Conze calls it, was seen as early as 300 B.C. and went on within Indian Buddhism for centuries. A Chinese writer of the seventh century estimates that at his time there were 60,000 Personalist monks, supporting the view that there is a 'self' in man, out of a total of 200,000 in the whole of India. The victory of the Non-Personalists within Buddhism may well have spelled defeat in the religious life of India, though the relentless opposition of the Brahmans and the invasion of Islam were also very powerful factors.

It will be interesting to follow the revival of Buddhism in India. During the recent celebrations of the 2500th

137

anniversary of the entry of the Buddha into Nirvana, the government and people of India took an outstanding part, and the Buddha was hailed as one of the greatest of India's sons. A number of leading people in public life have become Buddhists in recent years, including Dr Ambedkar, the leader of the Scheduled Classes, and Dr Niyogi, a well-known critic and opponent of Christianity. Dr Ambedkar's example has been followed by many thousands among the Scheduled Classes, who evidently think that social justice and human value are more likely to be inspired and secured through Buddhist principles. It should perhaps be added that very much larger numbers have joined the Christian Church over a long period, drawn by the vision of human value and a fellowship that transcends all human barriers. The influx of so many converts into Buddhism in India may well revive discussion of questions which seemed to have been settled in an earlier age.

The saying of the Buddha, 'There is an unborn, an unoriginated, unmade non-conditioned', is usually taken by Buddhists as referring to Nirvana. Christians would say that these terms are equally applicable to the conception of God, and should therefore be examined in this light. God and Nirvana are the two ultimates that have to be discussed in the Buddhist-Christian encounter.

Buddhist readers of this book will complain that the writer is obsessed by what they would describe as the illusion of the Eternal God. He would admit to the obsession, but would regret the word 'illusion'. The Christian would hold that Jesus went beyond the sphere

138

of form, the closed system of human life, that he unveiled a blind spot of Buddhism, in revealing a God, who is Creator and Redeemer, who is love as well as wisdom, who is the eternal SELF of all selfhood, who is personal, not in the sense that he suffers from man's limitations, but that he is the prototype in whose image man is made, that therefore he must be at least personal, since that is the highest relationship we know between men. The Christian would go further, in his conviction that the whole purpose of life, its goal and consummation is the vision of God. He would humbly admit that at present he only knows in part, but that there are times when he knows himself known and embraced by God. The journey through this life and the life after death is a preparation for the final vision, when at last the reality behind all the symbols under which we speak of God shall be seen and experienced in all its fulness. Buddhism is a magnificent preparation for that vision, but it stops short. Christ leads us not only through the veil of the temple to the presence of God himself, but through the cloud of unknowing, because he came from God and he returned to God, leading the human race on beyond its own furthest point of achievement, where God shall be all in all.

There in that other world what waits for me?
What shall I find after that other birth?
No stormy, tossing, foaming, smiling sea,
But a new earth.

No sun to mark the changing of the days,
No slow, soft falling of the alternate light,
No moon, no star, no light upon my ways,
      Only the Light.

No gray cathedral, wide and wondrous fair,
That I may tread where all my fathers trod,
Nay, nay, my soul, no house of God is there,
      But only God.[1]

[1] Mary E. Coleridge, *Poems 1908*.

Word-List of Buddhist Terms

Abhi-dhamma Lit. 'Beyond Dhamma'. One of the three main sections of the Pitakas (Buddhist Scriptures), dealing with psychological and philosophical categories.

Adi-Buddha The primeval or supreme Buddha thought by some Buddhists to have brought the world into being.

Anagami The Never Returner. The third stage in the attainment of Nirvana.

An-atta 'No soul, No self.' One of the three characteristics of human life as understood by Buddhists. In Thera-vada Buddhism, the denial of any personal immortal soul or self in man.

Anicca 'Impermanent.' The doctrine that everything is impermanent and subject to change. One of the three characteristics of being.

Arahant The personal ideal or saint in Thera-vada Buddhism. One who has become free from all desire and having thus attained to Nirvana will not be reborn.

Atman (Sanskrit.) The impersonal divine spirit either in the universe or in man (*atman*), as conceived in Hindu thought.

Bhikkhu 'Mendicant', 'homeless one'. A monk of the Thera-vada School.

Bodhi-sat (*Bodhisattra*). The ideal of the Mahayana School who has attained to Nirvana but stays on in the world for the sake of men.

Brahma The Ultimate Reality, according to Hindu thought; the impersonal Absolute.

Brahmanas The section of the Hindu Scriptures in which are preserved the details of ritual and sacrifice.

Brahmans The priestly caste in Indian life.

141

Buddha Awakened One, Enlightened One.

Dalai Lama The Spiritual and temporal ruler of Tibet; regarded as an incarnation of the Buddha. Now in India in exile.

Dhamma A difficult word to translate. It can mean Law, Teaching, Norm, Truth. The principle of order in the universe and in the moral sphere. Often used for the teaching of the Buddha. One of the Three Gems, with the Buddha and the Sangha.

Dukkha Lit. 'Pain, suffering'. Frustration, meaninglessness, unsubstantiality, emptiness. According to the Buddha one of the three characteristics of life.

Eightfold Path The way to eliminate desire: right view, thought, speech, action, livelihood, effort, mindfulness, concentration.

Five Precepts Not to take any life. Not to steal. Not to commit sexual impurity. Not to lie. Not to take intoxicants or drugs.

Four Noble Truths The Buddha's way of escape from *dukkha*. 1. Everything is marked by *dukkha*. 2. The cause is desire. 3. The cure is to eliminate desire. 4. The way to do this is to follow the Noble Eightfold Path.

Hina-yana 'Smaller or lower vehicle.' The name given by Mahayana Buddhists to the Thera-vada School as compared with Maha-yana, 'the great vehicle'. Better to use the term 'Thera-vada' or 'Southern'.

Jataka Birth story. There are 550 mythological birth stories of former incarnations of the Buddha.

Karma Lit. 'Action, doing'. The law of cause and effect, the logical consequence of deeds. 'As a man sows so does he reap.' Past deeds are productive of the present; present deeds are creative of the future.

Khandas Aggregates, constituents of being: body, feeling, perception, thought, consciousness.

Word-List of Buddhist Terms

Magga Path, Way.

Maha-yana Lit. 'The Great Vehicle'. The Northern School of Buddhism found in Tibet, China, Korea and Japan, which has many branches.

Maitreya (*Maitri*). The name of the final Buddha who is still to come.

Mantra Magical formula; right form of words in Hindu ritual.

Moksha Release, spiritual liberation.

Nirodha 'Stopping', the cessation of *dukkha*, through the stopping of desire.

Nirvana Lit. 'Blown out, become cool, extinct'. The goal of Buddhism: the perfection of being and blessing, when all desire has been extinguished, all fetters broken. Sometimes thought of in Thera-vada Buddhism as the annihilation of self as well as of desire.

Pali The language in which the Thera-vada Scriptures are written. It has many scripts. Most of the words in this glossary are Pali.

Pari-Nirvana Final or Total Nirvana, from which there is no return. This term is often used of the death of Buddha.

Pitakas 'Baskets.' The three main divisions of the Pali Scriptures:
 Vinaya or rules of the Order, the *Suttas* or Discourses, and the *Abhi-Dhamma* or philosophical treatises.

Sakadagami 'Once Returner', the second stage of the journey to Nirvana.

Samkhara One of the five *Khandas* or constituents of being – mental activities.

Samsara 'Wandering.' The endless round of rebirths on the earth; cycle of existence.

Samudaya 'Uprising', the cause of *dukkha*, which is desire.

Sangha The Buddhist Order of Monks. The third of the Three Gems, of which the other two are the Buddha himself and the Dhamma (Teaching).

Sañña Perception, one of the five aggregates of being.

Sotapanna 'Stream Entrant', the first stage in the realization of Nirvana.

Suttas 'Discourse, sermons.' The second 'basket' of the Pali Scriptures.

Tathagata 'One who has found the Truth.' Used of the Buddha: the Blessed One.

Thera Elder, monk. *Thera-gatha* – the Psalms of the Brethren.

Theri Sister, nun. *Theri-gatha* – the Psalms of the Sisters.

Thera-vada The doctrine of the Elders, considered to be the orthodox and original form of Buddhism, as followed in Ceylon and S.E. Asia. A more acceptable term than *Hina-yana*.

Three Gems The Buddha, the Dhamma and the Sangha, revered by all Buddhists, who begin every meditation with the threefold homage 'I go for reverence to the Buddha', etc.

Upanishads Lit. 'Sessions of instruction'. The philosophical section of the Hindu Scriptures.

Uposatha The fortnightly chapter at which each monk confesses his breaking of the rules of discipline.

Vedana Sensation, feeling. The second of the five *Khandas* or constituents of being.

Vedas The earliest of the Hindu Scriptures.

Vihara A retreat or monastery. Dwelling-place for the monks. (Sometimes used of a state of mind.)

Vinaya 'Discipline.' The first section of the Thera-vada Scriptures, dealing with Rules for the Monks.

Viññana Consciousness. The last of the five aggregates or constituents of being.

Yama, world of The underworld where men on death hear their fate. The Yamas or Watchers convey this judgement to them.

Word-List of Buddhist Terms

Yoga The Eastern disciple of meditation, combining exercises of breathing, posture and one-pointedness, and culminating in pure awareness.

Zen Japanese form of Pali *Jhana*, meditation. One of the main schools of Japanese Buddhism, emphasizing a form of meditation which transcends the mind in a direct experience of reality.

Books for Further Reading

Comparative Study of Religion

Appleton, G. *Glad Encounter* (Edinburgh House Press) 1959.

Dewick, E. C. *The Christian Attitude to Other Religions* (Cambridge University Press) 1953.

Gore, C. *The Philosophy of the Good Life* (Murray) 1930.

Kraemer, H. *Religion and the Christian Faith* (Lutterworth) 1956.

l'Anson Fausset, H. *The Flame and the Light* (Abelard-Schuman) 1958.

Otto, R. *Religious Essays* (Oxford University Press) 1931.

Zaehner, R. C. *At Sundry Times* (Faber & Faber) 1958.

Zaehner, R. C. (edited) *The Concise Encyclopaedia of Living Faiths* (Hutchinson) 1959.

The Psychological Approach

Fordham, F. *Introduction to Jung's Psychology* (Penguin) 1953.

James, Wm. *Varieties of Religious Experience* (Fontana) 1960.

Jung, C. G. *Modern Man in Search of a Soul* (Routledge & Kegan Paul) 1953.

Jung, C. G. *The Undiscovered Self* (Routledge & Kegan Paul) 1958

Martin, P. W. *Experiment in Depth* (Routledge & Kegan Paul) 1955.

Buddhism Generally

Conze, E. *Buddhism* (Cassirer) 1957.

Humphreys, C. *Studies in the Middle Way* 3rd ed. (Allen & Unwin) 1959.

Humphreys, C. *Buddhism* (Pelican) 1951.

Percheron, M. *Buddha and Buddhism* (Longmans) 1957.

Saunders, K. *The Story of Buddhism* (Oxford University Press) 1916.

Theravada Buddhism

Rahula, W. *What the Buddha Taught* (Gordon Fraser) 1959.

Rhys Davids, C. A. F. *Sakya* (Kegan Paul).

Rhys Davids, C. A. F. *Manual of Buddhism* (SPCK) 1932.

Ward, C. S. *Outline of Buddhism* (Epworth Press).

Mahayana Buddhism

Reichelt, K. L. *Truth and Tradition in Chinese Buddhism* (Shanghai) 1927.

Suzuki, D. T. *Introduction to Zen Buddhism* (Arrow Books) 1959.

Suzuki, D. T. *Manual of Zen Buddhism* (Rider) 1950.

Ward, C. S. *Mahayana Buddhism* (Epworth) 1952.

Watts, Alan *The Way of Zen* (Mentor Books) 1959.

Saunders, K. *The Gospel for Asia* (SPCK) 1928.

Buddhist Meditation

Conze, E. *Buddhist Meditation* (Allen & Unwin) 1956.

Nyanaponika Thera *The Heart of Buddhist Meditation* (Colombo) 1956.

Suzuki, D. T. *Mysticism: Christian and Buddhist* (Allen & Unwin) 1957.

Buddhist Scriptures

For Texts and Translations the series published by the Pali Text Society and The Sacred Books of the East (Oxford).

Books for Further Reading

Buddhist Texts through the Ages. Edited by E. Conze, I. B. Horner, D. Snellgrove, A. Waley (Cassirer) 1954.

Buddhist Scripture. Translated by E. Conze (Penguin) 1959.

Some Sayings of the Buddha. Translated by F. L. Woodward (Oxford University Press) 1939.

The Living Thoughts of Gotama the Buddha. A. K. Coomaraswamy and I. B. Horner (Cassell) 1948.

The Quest of Enlightenment. E. J. Thomas (Murray) 1950.

Index

151

Index

Conze, Edward, 101, 136, 137
Coomaraswamy, A. K., 20, 120
Coulson, C. A., 62, 63
Cross, the, 69, 80

DACOITY, 98
Dalai Lama, 83
Davids, Mrs Rhys, 20, 29, 79, 112, 119
Davids, T. W., 119
death, 56, 82, 86
deathlessness, 24, 110
democracy, 16
de Silva, Lynn A., 47, 135
desire, 32f, 36, 77, 82, 87, 89, 91, 96, 126
detachment, 107
Devas, 112, 114, 120
Dhamma (truth), 33, 36, ch. 3 *passim*, 61, 63, 64, 77, 96, 104, 106, 110, 135
  -pada, 25, 26, 32, 58, 78, 105
  and *Torah*, 44f
Dingle, Herbert, 62
discipleship, 69
dreams, 83
Dukkha (emptiness), 33, 34, 35, ch. 4 *passim*, 55, 76, 87, 89

ECCLESIASTES, 35, 54, 77, 92f
Eckhart, Meister, 72, 132, 133
Edinburgh World Missionary Conference (1910), 16f, 18

Ego, the, 67, 69, 129
Eliot, T. S., 52f
Enlightened One. *See* Buddha
Enlightenment, the, 85, 110
eternal life, 131
eternity, 132, 133
existence of God, 126, 137

FAUSSET L'ANSON, 59, 63, 77
Five Great Commands, 97, 104, 124
Fordham, Frieda, 66
forgiveness, Christian doctrine of, 80, 81

GAIRDNER, TEMPLE, 18
Gandhi, 49
Gautama. *See* Buddha
Genesis, 128
God, as Creator and Redeemer, 139
  belief in, 126ff, 138
grace, 130
Guardini, R., 23, 38f

HEBREWS, EPISTLE TO THE, 92
Hell, in Buddhism, 111
Hinduism, Hindus, 29, 30, 31, 66, 67, 127, 133
Hiroshima, 49
Holy Spirit, the, 74, 116, 133
Horner, I. B., 20, 120
Hort, Dr, 43
Humphreys, Christmas, 64

IMAGE OF GOD IN MAN, THE, 73, 74, 103, 128, 130
Independence, 15

Index